THE SHOCKING TRUTH ABOUT NORTH KOREAN TYRANNY

HEARING

BEFORE THE

SUBCOMMITTEE ON ASIA AND THE PACIFIC

OF THE

COMMITTEE ON FOREIGN AFFAIRS
HOUSE OF REPRESENTATIVES

ONE HUNDRED THIRTEENTH CONGRESS

SECOND SESSION

MARCH 26, 2014

Serial No. 113–132

Printed for the use of the Committee on Foreign Affairs

Available via the World Wide Web: http://www.foreignaffairs.house.gov/ or
http://www.gpo.gov/fdsys/

U.S. GOVERNMENT PRINTING OFFICE

87–337PDF   WASHINGTON : 2014

COMMITTEE ON FOREIGN AFFAIRS

EDWARD R. ROYCE, California, *Chairman*

CHRISTOPHER H. SMITH, New Jersey
ILEANA ROS-LEHTINEN, Florida
DANA ROHRABACHER, California
STEVE CHABOT, Ohio
JOE WILSON, South Carolina
MICHAEL T. McCAUL, Texas
TED POE, Texas
MATT SALMON, Arizona
TOM MARINO, Pennsylvania
JEFF DUNCAN, South Carolina
ADAM KINZINGER, Illinois
MO BROOKS, Alabama
TOM COTTON, Arkansas
PAUL COOK, California
GEORGE HOLDING, North Carolina
RANDY K. WEBER SR., Texas
SCOTT PERRY, Pennsylvania
STEVE STOCKMAN, Texas
RON DeSANTIS, Florida
DOUG COLLINS, Georgia
MARK MEADOWS, North Carolina
TED S. YOHO, Florida
LUKE MESSER, Indiana

ELIOT L. ENGEL, New York
ENI F.H. FALEOMAVAEGA, American
  Samoa
BRAD SHERMAN, California
GREGORY W. MEEKS, New York
ALBIO SIRES, New Jersey
GERALD E. CONNOLLY, Virginia
THEODORE E. DEUTCH, Florida
BRIAN HIGGINS, New York
KAREN BASS, California
WILLIAM KEATING, Massachusetts
DAVID CICILLINE, Rhode Island
ALAN GRAYSON, Florida
JUAN VARGAS, California
BRADLEY S. SCHNEIDER, Illinois
JOSEPH P. KENNEDY III, Massachusetts
AMI BERA, California
ALAN S. LOWENTHAL, California
GRACE MENG, New York
LOIS FRANKEL, Florida
TULSI GABBARD, Hawaii
JOAQUIN CASTRO, Texas

AMY PORTER, *Chief of Staff*   THOMAS SHEEHY, *Staff Director*
JASON STEINBAUM, *Democratic Staff Director*

SUBCOMMITTEE ON ASIA AND THE PACIFIC

STEVE CHABOT, Ohio, *Chairman*

DANA ROHRABACHER, California
MATT SALMON, Arizona
MO BROOKS, Alabama
GEORGE HOLDING, North Carolina
SCOTT PERRY, Pennsylvania
DOUG COLLINS, Georgia
LUKE MESSER, Indiana

ENI F.H. FALEOMAVAEGA, American
  Samoa
AMI BERA, California
TULSI GABBARD, Hawaii
BRAD SHERMAN, California
GERALD E. CONNOLLY, Virginia
WILLIAM KEATING, Massachusetts

CONTENTS

THE SHOCKING TRUTH ABOUT NORTH KOREAN TYRANNY

WEDNESDAY, MARCH 26, 2014

House of Representatives,
Subcommittee on Asia and the Pacific,
Committee on Foreign Affairs,
Washington, DC.

The committee met, pursuant to notice, at 2 o'clock p.m., in room 2172 Rayburn House Office Building, Hon. Steve Chabot (chairman of the subcommittee) presiding.

Mr. CHABOT. The hearing will come to order. Good afternoon. I am chairman of the Asia and Pacific Subcommittee, and I'd like to yield my time to the chairman of the full committee, Ed Royce of California.

Mr. ROYCE. I thank the gentleman for yielding, and I want to welcome our witnesses. I think my good friend, Steve Chabot, has done a lot of work over the years, and holding this important and timely hearing is part of that effort to make certain that we see some justice for people who have been through things which are unimaginable for us here.

I want to take the opportunity to welcome Ms. Minhee Jo to the Foreign Affairs Committee, and to thank her for bravely sharing her story. And I want to also share, as chairman of the Foreign Affairs Committee, that it's my commitment to all the people who continue to suffer in North Korea that this committee will do all it can Kim Jong-un and his generals accountable for crimes against humanity.

Today, I am announcing that the committee plans to consider bipartisan sanctions legislation against North Korea which I authored in May of this year. My legislation targets the regime where it is most vulnerable, in the pocketbook, and it will prevent Kim Jong-un from assessing or accessing, having the ability to use that hard currency that he needs in order to pay his generals.

H.R. 1771 now has over 130 cosponsors, and it will go a long way toward bankrupting the regime in North Korea.

It is important that we wake up to the reality that North Korea is not interested in reform. Frankly, that's not—denuclearization does not drive their calculus. And, thus, I urge the administration to work with this committee so that the people of North Korea can finally have an opportunity to live without fear, to have an existence without abuse.

And I've long been involved in shining the spotlight on the horrific human rights abuses in North Korea. I've had many, many trips to that part of the world and spoken with so many defectors about their particular circumstances. I've had people show me the scars on their bodies from when they tortured in North Korea.

I co-chair the International Parliamentarians Coalition for North Korean Refugees and Human Rights, and I can say that the Committee of Inquiry Report on North Korea offers one of the most comprehensive accountings of human rights abuses in that country.

Despite the international community's focus on North Korea's weapons program over the past 20 years, too little attention is paid to the question of human rights, the lack of human rights in the country. And this report has finally changed the way the world views North Korea, and I'm hopeful that with this new awareness action is not far behind.

Last month I led a bipartisan delegation to Seoul. I've been there many times, but this is the second time in some 12 months in order to reaffirm our nation's special alliance with South Korea. In my meetings with President Park, she has always stressed the importance of fighting, struggling for human rights for the people of North Korea. She said it last year, and she said it again this year to us.

As a longtime friend of the Korean people, I know that this issue is very important to South Koreans and Korean Americans alike, and that's why I'm committed to passing this legislation into law, and also because I've looked into the eyes of those who have survived in North Korea. And I want to make certain that that type of horrific thing does not continue to occur.

Fighting for human rights is one of the most important tasks that we have as a nation, and that we have here as members of this committee. When we see grave abuses occurring it is our duty to stand up and take action.

Chairman Chabot, thank you for your leadership on this issue, and I look forward to hearing the testimonies of this distinguished panel.

Mr. CHABOT. Thank you, Mr. Chairman. And the chair announces that we have a series of votes on the floor. The buzzers that you heard going off were to call us over to the floor to vote, so we're going to go over and vote right now. Then we'll come back and finish opening statements, we'll hear from the panel, and have time for questions, and that sort of thing. So, we apologize for any inconvenience, but we have to head over and vote. We'll be back in a short period of time. The committee is in recess.

[Recess.]

Mr. CHABOT. Welcome, everyone, to this afternoon's Asia and Pacific Subcommittee hearing on the shocking truth about North Korean tyranny. I want to thank my colleague from California, Mr. Ami Bera, for serving as today's ranking member and also thank our distinguished witnesses for being here, as well. We're especially extremely grateful to Ms. Grace Jo, as the chairman mentioned before, that you could join us here this afternoon. Your perspective will be invaluable for everyone to hear today. I'll make my formal introductions of all the witnesses after I've concluded and the ranking member has concluded his opening statements here this afternoon.

We've already heard from the full committee chairman, Mr. Royce, but we had to go into recess because of votes. We won't have any votes for another hour and half or so, I don't think, so hopefully we can get through the rest of the hearing before we have votes again.

For 60 years, North Korea has been ruled by one of the most repressive totalitarian regimes on earth. Millions of North Koreans have been starved to death and sent to concentration camps to die in inhumane ways not seen since the days of Hitler or Stalin. The extent of human rights abuses, a list too long to go into great detail, are deliberate and calculated actions utilized by the Kim regime to quell dissent and maintain ultimate control, just as his father and grandfather did before him.

In February, the United Nations Commission of Inquiry released its report on human rights in North Korea, yielding a compendium of crimes against humanity committed by the North Korean regime. While the totality of this report is certainly shocking—a wake up call for the international community to take action—the horrors described are not a surprise to the human rights community, which has worked with dozens of individuals who have been lucky enough to escape from the Kim chamber of horrors. Yet, North Korea remains one of the least understood regimes in a world seemingly focused elsewhere.

As discussions at the U.N. about the Commission of Inquiry Report continue throughout this week in Geneva, I would urge the international community to reach a consensus to do more than just condemn by words. The time for willful blindness, for looking the other way for North Korea's abuses must come to an end. There is a tremendous amount the international community can and must do. Future discussions about North Korea should make human rights a priority right alongside nuclear disarmament.

North Korea has consistently represented one of the greatest security challenges for the United States because of its determined pursuit of nuclear weapons and missiles. But the threat North Korea poses to our South Korean ally, its record of human rights abuses and the dangers that it presents to regional stability make dealing with North Korea that much more difficult. After decades of trying to negotiate, cajole, and pressure North Korea to halt its proliferation and stand by its commitments, we have seen little success. In fact, North Korea seems much more determined today to act irresponsibly than ever before.

Since 2009, the U.S. has pursued a reactive policy toward North Korea called "Strategic Patience," which maintains leveled pressure and resolute warnings with a door to renewed discussions partly open. This policy, however, has not slowed North Korea's nuclear program, as illustrated by Pyongyang's decision to restart its Yongbyon reactor, and as has been noted in the recently released U.N. Panel of Experts Report, North Korea continues to develop creative ways to evade U.N. Security Council prohibitions on trade and economic activities to boost its nuclear and missile programs. It has also done nothing to decrease the extent of human rights violations in North Korea. Clearly, U.S. policy has been ineffective.

Since Kim Jong-un assumed power in December 2011, he has embraced the evil, tyrannical, depraved, corrupt, and vile characteristics of his father and grandfather. Despite only slight stylistical leadership differences, the ultimate goals for North Korea remain the same and the pursuit of nuclear weapons continues unfettered.

Throughout 2012 and 2013, the world witnessed an escalation of war-like rhetoric and dangerously irresponsible actions from the third-generation Kim, who wanted nothing more than to show the world his threats were real. And this bellicose behavior continues. During this year's joint U.S.-South Korea military drills, which began in February, North Korea conducted a number of prohibited missile tests. Just this past weekend, North Korea test fired 46 short-range rockets, bringing the total to 70 over the course of the last month, one of which came within range of a Chinese passenger plane. Pyongyang has claimed these tests as part of its own routine self-defense exercises.

The Obama administration appears to have outsourced its North Korean policy to China, but China's policies, too, are failing. The sudden and brutal removal of Jang Sung Taek thought to be close to Beijing, was a blow to China, and now the Kim regime seems to be trying to push China out of its circle of influence. This raises a number of concerns and questions as to how China will act in the coming months as the U.S. urges Beijing to not veto the inevitable Security Council resolution condemning North Korea's human rights record, and to stop evading our sanctions policy by funneling money to support Pyongyang's nuclear and missile production.

It's clear that a non-nuclear and compliant North Korea is an unreachable goal if the administration maintains its current policy approach. We cannot become comfortably accustomed to North Korea's possession of nuclear weapons or its systematic torture and killing of its own people.

North Korea is a grave threat to the United States and our allies in Asia. Policies pursued by Presidents of both parties, with minor variations, have failed. It is time for us to reconsider the policies that haven't worked, and reapply those that have. Trading valuable concessions failed once, so let's not ''buy the same horse twice.'' I believe it's possible to disarm North Korea involuntarily without the use of force. Legislation was introduced last year to give the President the legal tools to do just that. The U.N.'s report makes it vividly clear that if the world community continues to dawdle, growing numbers of innocent North Koreans will suffer and die in horrific ways. Now is the time to put our resources together and act.

I look forward to our witness' testimonies this afternoon, and discussing options we have to hold the North Korean regime accountable. At this time, I would like to turn to the acting ranking member of the committee, Ami Bera from California.

Mr. BERA. Thank you, Chairman Chabot. And thank you for calling this incredibly important hearing to discuss North Korea's abysmal human rights record, and clearly the other serious issues that are taking place as North Korea postures.

As we all know and we've talked about in the past, North Koreans are deprived of just the basic fundamental freedoms and universal human rights for decades. North Koreans don't have freedom of speech, they don't have freedom of movement, they don't have freedom of religion, and they're also subjected to chronic starvation and abysmal and dismal public health system.

Last month, the U.N. released a disturbing report on the gross human rights violations and oppression that North Koreans experience under the Kim regime. The U.N. report details atrocious crimes against humanity that are occurring every day, such as persecution, murder, sexual abuse, and forced abortion. However, the perpetrators of these horrendous crimes remain immune by the North Korean justice system, which is utterly despicable.

Unless rampant immunity is addressed and stopped, these egregious violations against humanity will, unfortunately, continue in North Korea. I'm also very concerned with North Korean's aggressive behavior toward South Korea, its nuclear weapons program, and the security threat it poses to the region.

Just last Saturday, as the chairman mentioned, North Korea launched 30 short-range rockets into open waters to demonstrate its discontent with ongoing U.S.-South Korea military exercises. This morning North Korea fired two mid-range missiles in Japan's direction in protest for trilateral talks that were held between the U.S., Japan, and South Korea.

These types of provocations are completely unacceptable and threaten to destabilize the region. As the world's greatest democracy, we must take a tougher stance with our international partners on North Korea's threatening antics and deplorable human rights record.

Lastly, I want to highlight the importance of strengthening our partnership and our relationship with South Korea. In 2013, South Korea was the United States' sixth largest trading partner. According to the California Chamber of Commerce, California is Korea's fifth largest export destination, and in 2013 exported nearly $8.4 billion of product to South Korea. It's an incredibly important relationship.

Korean Americans also have a very deep-seated history and deep-seated roots in my home state of California. The vibrant and thriving Korean community has successfully created two of the largest cultural heritage centers outside of Korea in both Los Angeles and Oakland. Deepening our longstanding friendship and cooperative relationship with South Korea is imperative and necessary as we look to stabilize the inter-Korean relationship.

I look forward to reviewing our positions, and I remain wholeheartedly committed in supporting a peaceful and prosperous Pacific region.

Mr. Chairman, I'd like to thank you again for calling this crucial hearing, and I look forward to the testimony of our witnesses.

Mr. CHABOT. Thank you very much. And now are there any other members who would like to make a brief opening statement? I'll recognize the gentleman from California, Mr. Rohrabacher.

Mr. ROHRABACHER. Thank you very much, Mr. Chairman, for holding this hearing and let the word go forth that the Congress of the United States understands the monstrous nature of the regime that now controls North Korea.

North Korea's military power has been financed by taking food from its people, medicine from its sick, education from its children. They have used that wealth that should have gone to supply just basic needs for their people, and instead used it to subsidize a ghoulish elite that is guilty of monstrous crimes, and to subsidize a military power that would then, of course, be used not only for their country's security against threats from abroad, but also be used against its own people to keep themselves in power.

The North Korea horror story is testimony to the failure of a policy that is based on trying to change the behavior of some monstrous gangster regimes by treating them well, or by doing them favors, or trying to figure out a way of being nice to them thinking that that will change the fundamental nature, or in some way affect the decisions of those people who rule with an iron fist as far as North Korea.

Mr. Chairman, I'm not sure if you were here then or not, but I certainly remember a debate in which I sat right over here years ago about whether or not we should be providing North Korea with energy, with oil, and whether we should help feed their population. And, of course, over a decade we provided huge amounts of food and energy for the North Korea Government and surprise, surprise, it didn't change the nature of that horrible regime. It didn't civilize the leaders of that country whatsoever. And today we, in fact, can see no results whatsoever to the hundreds of millions of dollars of humanitarian assistance that we gave to the people of North Korea, yet they are still held in bondage and their government—it has had no impact on their government policies whatsoever.

We need to take this as a lesson, make sure that it guides what our decisions are in the future, which is we should be siding with the oppressed rather than trying to curry favor with the oppressor. And we have not reached out to the people of North Korea in an effort to eliminate that horrible regime that oppresses them, so I look forward to hearing more details about what's happening in North Korea from our witnesses.

Mr. CHABOT. Thank you. Mr. Rohrabacher, by the way, is the chairman of the Europe, Eurasia, and Emerging Threats Subcommittee. I'd now like to recognize another gentleman from California. We've got a lot of Californians here this afternoon. Brad Sherman, who is the ranking member of the Terrorism, Nonproliferation, and Trade Subcommittee. The gentleman is recognized.

Mr. SHERMAN. Mr. Chairman, it was good to be with you, the chairman of the full committee, and others on our trip to Asia last month where we had a chance to meet with President Park, to view the DMZ, and even a few soldiers of the North Korea military. And one thing that's striking because I think it's the only place in the world where this is true, land is considerably cheaper in Northern Seoul than Southern Seoul simply because in Northern Seoul you're under the gun of more than tens of thousands of artillery pieces north of the DMZ. I think Seoul is the only great city in the world where you have a national security reason for land to be cheaper on one side of town than the other side of town.

The gentleman from California makes a point about our aid. I would say that were there to be a curtailment and rollback of the nuclear program of North Korea, that might not help the people of North Korea, but it would make this a safer planet. And I would differ with him under those circumstances which do not exist and, therefore, don't differ with him.

You know, I've served on this committee for about 18 years. We've heard every possible description of cruelty, but this is a nationwide gulag. This isn't some people being oppressed, this is virtually everyone. And this will go down in history as one of the cruelest regimes in the world, certainly the cruelest in Korean history.

We should keep in mind that this regime survives only because of the subsidy it receives from China. And on a trade policy that gives China—allows China to sell $300 billion more in the United States than we sell there empowers Beijing, and Beijing doesn't always use that power for good.

Kim Jong-un has simply added an element of immaturity and mercurial unpredictability, and instability to what was already a cruel regime.

And, finally, we should never hesitate to call on Japan, and especially South Korea to spend more on its military. We who are blessed to behind oceans and are not on the front lines spend over 5 percent of our GDP on our military if you include veterans benefits, as I do, whereas South Korea spends roughly 2.7 percent, Japan slightly less than 1 percent. And those who are on the front lines who face the greatest threat should be willing to spend as much of their treasure as we do. I yield back.

Mr. CHABOT. I thank the gentleman, and I'd at this time like to introduce our distinguished panel.

We begin with Grace Jo who was born in North Korea, a place where she almost starved to death as a child. In 2006, Ms. Jo and two of her family members escaped North Korea. Soon after, she and her family were rescued by the United Nations High Commissioner for Refugees which enabled them to enter the U.S. as legal refugees. Grace is one of 170 refugees from North Korea who have settled in the U.S. She became a U.S. citizen last year and we congratulate you for that, and welcome you. Grace lives outside of Washington, DC. She and her family have actively protested the forced repatriation of North Korean escapees hiding out in China. In addition to being a human rights activist, she dreams of going to law school to study international law for the purpose of helping North Korean defectors. Ms. Jo works as a dental certified assistant in the United Dental Group to earn a living. She attends classes in the evening to reach her academic goals. She also volunteers for her sister's nonprofit organization, North Korea in USA, which helps North Korean refugees in the United States and China. And we welcome you here.

I would next like to introduce Greg Scarlatoiu. Mr. Scarlatoiu is the executive director for the Committee for Human Rights in North Korea (HRNK) where he handles outreach programs aiming to focus world attention on human rights abuses in North Korea. Prior to joining HRNK, he was the director of public affairs and business issues of the Korea Economic Institute. He has also served as management associate for the International Science and Technology Institute in Arlington, Virginia. He previously lived in Seoul for 10 years and is fluent in Korean, French, and Rumanian. He has also authored a weekly radio column broadcast by Radio Free Asia to North Korea. Mr. Scarlatoiu holds master's in international relations from Tufts University Fletcher School of Law and Diplomacy, and Seoul National University, and a B.A. in international relations from Seoul National University. Mr. Scarlatoiu was conferred the title of Citizen of Honor, City of Seoul and is also a member of the board of directors for the International Council on Korean Studies, and we welcome you here this afternoon.

We also have Bruce Klingner who is the senior research fellow for Northeast Asia at the Heritage Foundation's Asian Study Center. Previously, he served as the CIA's Deputy Division Chief for Korea where he provided analysis on political, military, economic, and leadership issues for the President of the United States and other senior U.S. policymakers. He was the Chief of CIA's Korea Branch, which analyzed military developments during a nuclear crisis with North Korea. Mr. Klingner is a distinguished graduate of the National War College where he received a master's degree in national security strategy. He also holds a master's degree in strategic intelligence from the Defense Intelligence College and a bachelor's degree in political science from Middlebury College in Vermont.

And, as I said, we welcome all three witnesses here this afternoon. We have, of course, what you probably heard referred to as the 5-minute rule. There are lights down there that will let you know when you have 1 minute to go, it will turn yellow at that point, and when it turns red, we ask that you wrap it up. Your time is up at that point. We'll also limit ourselves to 5 minutes in asking questions. So, we'll begin with you this afternoon, Ms. Jo, and you probably need to turn the mic on there. Thank you.

STATEMENT OF MS. GRACE JO, SURVIVOR OF NORTH KOREAN HUMAN RIGHTS ABUSES

Ms. Jo. Thank you very much. Hello, my name is Grace Jo. It's very nice to see everyone here.

I was born in 1991 in North Hamkyoung Province in North Korea. In 1993, our family started to have shortage of food. In 1997 to 1998 my family was my father, maternal grandmother, younger siblings and big sister.

Since I was born, my parents have tried many different ways to raise us. They tried to find sustenance in wild vegetables, grasshoppers, rats, tree barks and even cattle in government-operated farms. In North Korea killing a cow is considered a crime comparable to homicide, so a person caught killing a cow could be sentenced to death by shooting.

Fully aware of these facts, my parents risked their lives in order to feed my family. Our family did everything we could try but due to the government's prohibition you cannot do any business, and eventually even my parents ran out of ways to feed our family. They made the hard decision to illegally cross the border to China. In Spring 1997, my parents illegally visited a relative in China and purchased some food with their help.

However, when they arrived home, my father was arrested by the police, and officials of our home town came with clubs and took my mother away after ruthlessly beating her. They also took away all of the food. My grandmother, my younger brother, my older sister, and I all cried as we tried to hold on to the things that they were taking away. In 1 day we lost our parents and our food, and our house was in ruins with nothing left for us. Later, we learned afterwards that my father had told the officials about my mother's pregnancy and begged for her release. However, my father admitted all the charges that they were accusing him of and he was punished.

Because he was a man, he had to suffer from all kinds of torture by the police. In the end, while he was being transported to a prison on a train he passed away unable to stand any further.

Continuously, many things happened that led us to leave our hometown and escape to China. However, we were deported back to North Korea four times. When we were sent back to North Korea, I myself did not receive too many punishments since I was a minor. However, the miseries I saw ripped at my heart. When minors are sent back to North Korea, Bo-Wee-Bu take them to orphanages called Koo-Ho-So. The first orphanage I was sent to was located in Sinuiju. In Sinuiju, among the people who are staying at the orphanage included a 5-week-old infant to an 18-year-old. The directors at the orphanage gave only 40 gram of baby formula per day. Sixteen-year-olds were less than four feet tall. There were two groups of children at the orphanage. The first group was those few children who had enough strength to go out to the market field and steal food. And there were those who could only stay inside of the orphanage. Those who could move built storage rooms and did other labor.

Inside the orphanage there were about 10 rooms and 15 to 20 children stayed in each room. The space was so small that everyone had to sleep in the same direction at night. There wasn't enough water. And for food, instead of rice, we were given barley and radish soup.

After waking up at 6 each morning, we had to work until 7 p.m. For the smallest instance, the directors would punish us. And because guards stood post every day, we couldn't escape outside the orphanage over the wall. For an example, a 15-year-old who was caught escaping tore his left leg tendon as a result of a beating. And there was no one to take care of his condition. Some of these children who were beaten had their food taken away and worked endlessly, died because of their weakness.

I am 5 foot 3 inches, but when I was sent back to North Korea in 2006, they used to call me a giant. And one time I was slapped on the face on account of my height. Likewise, many others born in and after the '90s couldn't grow due to malnutrition.

Education was available only for those children from families with good backgrounds, with ties to the government, and with ties to Communist heroes. Only those from families who did well enough to give money or other goods to the teachers or schools could attend schools. The study materials available were in poor quality, such as paper made from tree barks for writing.

Lastly, in October 2006, there were three boiled potatoes that the orphanage was giving out to the children. Our family, before being released, was staying together for 3 days at an orphanage after transported to my hometown. And when we asked the girl who brought the potatoes to us, she said they had been living on those potatoes for the past 2 weeks. I was well over 10 years old, but North Korea had not changed at all during my lifetime.

A country that beats people to death like they are animals for having a religion, a country that sends a family of three generations for one family member's trivial comment, a country that requires a travel permit for someone to attend his or her parent's funeral, in novels, books, biographies, and poems, nothing else can be written but praises of the Great Leader. It is a country with absolutely no freedom, a country that abuses its senior citizens and mistreats its children while it labels them as ''treasures.'' A country that has beaten its citizens for the past over 20 years, a country in which the soldiers rob the civilians of their food. I believe in the U.S. and the U.N., a country and an international body that actually do treat the children as they should be as ''treasures.'' I would like to please ask the U.S. and U.N. to rescue the suffering North Korean people.

I would like to please ask you, please remember the Holocaust. At least the survivors have finally found their freedom, and may live freely as all of you do. However, the people in North Korea have been living under tyranny over the past several decades, and even right now, as the people suffered under the Nazi regime. Please be their voice, and be advocates of their human rights. Thank you very much.

[The prepared statement of Ms. Jo follows:]

Human Rights Abuses in North Korea:

A Survivor's Perspective

Testimony before

House Foreign Affairs Committee

Subcommittee on Asia & the Pacific

"The Shocking Truth about

North Korean Tyranny"

March 26, 2014

Grace Minhee Jo

Survivor of North Korean Human Rights Abuses

Mr. Chairman, ranking member, and members of the Subcommittee, please accept my sincere appreciation for the opportunity to testify before the subcommittee today. My name is Minhee Jo. I was born in 1991 in North Hamkyoung Province, in North Korea. (We were protected under UNHCR for about a year in Beijing, China, and upon receiving refugee status, my family came directly to the United States on March 20th, 2008.) The story of my family is as follows.

Starting in 1993, our family started to have shortage of food. In 1997, my family lost my father, maternal grandmother, younger siblings, and big sister. Since I was born, my parents have tried many different ways to raise me and my siblings. We tried to find sustenance in wild vegetables, grasshoppers, rats, tree barks, and even cattle in government-operated farms. In North Korea, killing a cow is considered a crime comparable to homicide, so a person caught killing a cow could be sentenced to death by shooting. Full aware of these facts, my parents risked their lives in order to feed my family. Our family did everything we could try, but due to the government's prohibition, we could not do any business, and eventually when my parents ran out of ways to feed our family, they made the hard decision to illegally cross the border to China. In Spring, 1997, my parents illegally visited a relative in China and purchased some food with their help.

However, when they arrived home, my father was arrested by the police, and officials of our town came with clubs and took my mother away after ruthlessly beating her. They also took away all of the food. My grandmother, my younger brother who couldn't walk at the time, my older sister, and I all cried as we tried to hold on to the things that they were taking away. In one day, we lost our parents and our food, and our house was in ruins with nothing left for us.

My grandmother cursed this world, and there wasn't anything that any of us children could do other than crying and staring at the road where we last saw our mother being taken away. We survived each day on wild plants and water as we earnestly waited for our parents' return. Three months passed, and we could finally see the contour of my mother coming back through the woods. We all ran towards her and greeted her with tears and hugs, filled with joy. She could barely walk due to the tortures she had suffered. Her body was all bruised, and she just lay on the floor, unable to get up, for about a month. In her conversation with my grandmother, I could hear all the tortures she had to undergo.

When she was jailed, she was forced to sit still, not allowed to move. They stepped on her legs as she sat still. They made her put forward her hands so that they could step on them with their heels. As a result, she couldn't use her legs. Although she said that the tortures were not as bad as they could have been, at the time she had been pregnant for 3 months, so from our standpoint, they could have put her life in danger. We learned afterwards that my father had told the officials about my mother's pregnancy and begged for her release. It was thanks to him that we could see our mother again.

However, my father admitted all the charges that they were accusing him of, and he was punished. Because he was a man, he had to suffer from all kinds of torture by the police. Being kicked by the heels is only normal. They beat him with a club till it broke. And in order to hear the response that they wanted from my father, they forced him to starve for longer than 10 days with no water, tortured him, and beat him everyday. In the end, while he was being transported to a prison on a train, he passed away unable to withstand any further.

5 months after my mother was released, we heard the news of my father, and due to the shock, my mother bore a child at only 8 months. My youngest brother was born in the break of dawn with no light. My grandmother helped with the child-bearing, and all of us children were scared to death hearing my mother scream with pain.

Afterwards, many things happened that led us to leave our hometown and escape to China. However, we were deported back to North Korea 4 times, and it is still very difficult for me to explain the sort of torture and pain we suffered each time we were sent back. When we were sent back to North Korea, I myself did not receive too many punishments since I was a minor. However, the miseries I saw ripped my heart. When minors are sent back to North Korea, Bo-Wee-Bu (North Korean State Political Security Department) take them to orphanages called Koo-Ho-So ("Rescue Station") The first orphanage I was sent to was located in Sinuiju. The second was on Onsung-kun. In Sinuiju, among the people who were staying at the orphanage included a five-week-old infant to an 18 year-old. There was also a family of three, a mother and two daughters, who had lost their home due to fire. The directors at the orphanage gave only 40g (1.4 oz) of baby formula per day. 16 year-olds were less than 4 feet tall. There were two groups of children at the orphanage. The first group was those few children who had enough strength to go out to the market field and steal food. And there were those who could only stay inside the orphanage. Those who could move built storage rooms and did other labor. Inside the orphanage, there were about 10 rooms, and 15-20 children stayed in each room. The space was so small that everyone had to sleep in the same direction at night. There wasn't enough water. And for food, instead of rice, we were given barley and radish soup. We became hunger soon after eating. After waking up at 6 each morning, we had to work until 7pm, and we didn't receive any education. For the smallest incidents, the directors would punish us, and because guards stood post every day, we couldn't escape outside the orphanage over the wall. If someone was caught trying to escape, he or she was beaten until the instrument of beating broke. When a 15 year-old who was caught escaping tore his left leg tendon as a result of beating, and there was no one to take care of his condition. Some of these children who were beaten, had their food taken away, and worked endlessly died because of their weakness. I am 5'3, but when I was sent back to North Korea in 2006, they used to call me a giant, and one time, I was slapped on the face on account of my height. Likewise, many others born in and after the nineties couldn't grow due to malnutrition. Education was available only for those children from families with good backgrounds, with ties to the government, and with ties to communist heroes. Only those from families who did well enough to give money or other goods to the teachers or schools could attend schools. Children from families like ours that was caught after escaping from the country could only attend classes focused on ideological indoctrination, and the only study materials available were in poor quality such as "paper" made from tree barks for writing. At train stations and public places, there were young children sleeping under a bench as well as those children who had their clothes and shoes taken away by stronger kids. There were also those children who were suffering injuries from beating when they had been caught stealing food. Lastly, on October, 2006, there were three boiled potatoes that the orphanage was giving out to the children. Our family, before being released, was staying together for three days at an orphanage, and when we asked the girl who brought the potatoes to us, she said they had been living on those potatoes for the past two weeks. I was well over 10 years old, but North Korea had not changed at all during my lifetime.

A country that beats people to death like they are animals for having a religion, a country that sends a family of three generations for one family member's trivial comment, a country that requires a travel permit for someone to attend his or her parents' funeral… In novels, books, biographies, and poems, nothing else can be written but praises of the Great Leader. It is a country with absolutely no freedom. A country that abuses its senior citizens and mistreats its children though it labels them as "treasures." A country that has beaten its citizens for the past over 20 years. A country in which the soldiers rob the civilians of their food. I believe in the U.S. and the U.N., a country and an international body that actually do treat the children as they should be as "treasures." I would like to please ask the U.S. and U.N. to rescue the suffering North Korean people.

I would like to please ask you. Please remember the Holocaust. At least the survivors have finally found their freedom and may live freely as all of you do. However, the people in North Korea have been living under tyranny over the past several decades and even right now, as the people suffered under the Nazi regime. Please be their voice, and be advocates of their human rights.

There are many more stories I would like to share, but since the time is limited, I will conclude here. Thank you for your precious time, and thank you for listening.

Mr. CHABOT. Thank you very much for your testimony. Mr. Scarlatoiu, you're recognized for 5 minutes.

STATEMENT OF MR. GREG SCARLATOIU, EXECUTIVE DIRECTOR, COMMITTEE FOR HUMAN RIGHTS IN NORTH KOREA

Mr. SCARLATOIU. On behalf of the Committee for Human Rights in North Korea, I would like to express great appreciation to Chairman Steve Chabot and the distinguished members of the subcommittee for holding this hearing today to highlight the human rights situation in North Korea and for inviting me to testify. Mr. Chairman, in today's oral testimony I will be summarizing my written statement.

One hundred and twenty thousand men, women, and children, those suspected of being disloyal to the Kim regime and up to three generations of their families continue to be brutally persecuted behind the barbed wire fences of North Korea's political prison camps. The people of North Korea continue to be divided into three social categories and 51 subcategories based on their loyalty to the regime.

In the mid to late 1990s, as up to 3 million North Koreans starved to death, the Kim regime continued to invest in the development of its ballistic missile and nuclear weapons program. The human rights situation has deteriorated under the Kim Jong-un regime. Three trends stands out in particular, an aggressive crackdown on attempted defections, a forceful purge of former officials, and the restructuring of North Korea's political prison camp system, facilities near the border with China have been closed while other camps have been expanded.

The U.N. Commission of Inquiry on Human Rights in North Korea established by consensus by all 47 member states of the U.N. Human Rights Council found that in many instances the violations identified entailed crimes against humanity based on state policies. Systematic, widespread and gross human rights violations that have been and are being committed by North Korea involve extermination, murder, enslavement, torture, imprisonment, rape, forced abortions, and sexual violence, persecution on political, religious, racial, and gender grounds, the forcible transfer of populations, the enforced disappearance of persons, and the inhumane act of knowingly causing prolonged starvation.

The Commission of Inquiry determined that crimes against humanity target anyone viewed as a threat to the political system and leadership of North Korea, in particular, political prisoners, those attempting to defect, religious believers, Christians in particular, people introducing information from the outside world into North Korea, and citizens of other countries abducted by North Korea.

The Commission of Inquiry pointed out that since the Government of North Korea is not willing to prosecute its own officials, the United Nations will have to protect the population of North Korea and insure that those most responsible for crimes against humanity are held accountable.

The Commission of Inquiry further recommended that the U.N. Security Council refer the North Korean situation to the International Criminal Court. Furthermore, the inclusion of North Korean human rights in the U.N. Security Council's permanent agenda would be a long overdue and feasible measure.

It is our Committee for Human Rights in North Korea's view that the United States Government ought to support greater involvement by U.N. agencies in North Korea beyond the human rights bodies. U.N. agencies to which the United States Government is a significant contributor, agencies tasked with development of humanitarian assistance should be fully aware of the findings of the U.N. Commission of Inquiry and find ways to promote them.

U.S.-North Korea policy has been dominated by grave political security concerns. The policy of Strategic Patience has been one of very few, if any, options within a context defined by the North Korean regime's lack of international credibility and established patterns of deceitful behavior.

Nevertheless, crimes against humanity have been and are being committed in North Korea.

As the horror of what author Mark Helprin termed as a ''slow motion holocaust continues,'' the people and the Government of the United States can unambiguously afford no Strategic Patience that would allow the Kim regime more time to abuse, starve, wrongfully imprison, maim, torture, and kill the innocent.

Human rights concerns must be included in the agenda of future bilateral and multilateral talks with North Korea should such talks be resumed. The international sanctions regime against North Korea aims to prevent the development and proliferation of weapons of mass destruction and ballistic missile technology by North Korea, and is not linked to North Korea's human rights situation.

In order to achieve international momentum on a scale comparable to the anti-apartheid campaign of the 1980s, the international sanctions regime must address North Korea's human rights violations.

A sanctions regime effectively addressing the North Korean human rights situation must sever access to funds linked to the crimes against humanity and other human rights violations perpetrated by the North Korean regime until the situation has been verifiably remedied. Effective sanctions should also sever the access to luxury goods and foreign travel for those officials most responsible for North Korea's crimes against humanity.

Mr. Chairman, the Committee for Human Rights in North Korea considers it essential to bring attention to the systematic widespread crimes against humanity, and egregious human rights violations perpetrated by the North Korea regime to protect the victims, to bring justice to their tormentors, and without further delay to seek ways to improve the human rights situation in that country. Thank you very much.

[The prepared statement of Mr. Scarlatoiu follows:]

Statement of Greg Scarlatoiu, Executive Director, Committee for Human Rights in North Korea (HRNK): "The Shocking Truth about North Korean Tyranny," Hearing of the U.S. House of Representatives Committee on Foreign Affairs, Subcommittee on Asia and the Pacific

On behalf of the Committee for Human Rights in North Korea (HRNK), I would like to express great appreciation to Chairman Steve Chabot for holding this hearing today to highlight the human rights situation in North Korea, and for inviting me to testify. The Committee for Human Rights in North Korea considers it essential to bring attention to the systematic, widespread crimes against humanity and egregious human rights violations perpetrated by the North Korean regime, to protect the victims, to bring justice to their tormentors, and, without further delay, to seek ways to improve the human rights situation in that country.

The Committee for Human Rights in North Korea (HRNK)

HRNK is a US-based, bipartisan organization, established in 2001, to conduct research, publish reports and carry out outreach activities to focus international attention on the human rights situation in North Korea. For more than a decade, the organization's well documented and well written studies have established its reputation and leading role in the international network of organizations committed to promoting human rights in North Korea and to designing solutions for improving the situation. Its report *The Hidden Gulag: Exposing North Korea's Prison Camps* (2003, 2012 and 2013) was the first to fully put on the map the North Korean political prison camp system through interviews with former prisoners, guards, and government officials formerly in charge of running the camps as well as satellite images.

The North Korean Human Rights Situation

For more than 65 years, North Korea's human rights record has been abysmal. A quarter century after the collapse of communism in the former Soviet Union and Eastern Europe, North Korea's Kim regime has maintained its tyrannical grip on power, while accomplishing two hereditary transmissions of power: from Kim Il-sung to Kim Jong-il in July 1994, and from Kim Jong-il to Kim Jong-un in December 2011. The primary strategic objective of the Kim regime continues to be its own self-preservation, regardless of the toll imposed on the North Korean people's fundamental human rights.

Although North Korea is bound, as a UN member state, by the *Universal Declaration of Human Rights,* and although it is a party to the *International Covenant on Civil and Political Rights,* the *International Covenant on Economic, Social, and Cultural Rights,* the *Convention on the Rights of the Child,* the *Genocide Convention,* and the *Convention on the Elimination of All Forms of Discrimination against Women,* each and every conceivable human right continues to be violated in that country. In the year 2014, 120,000 men, women, and children, continue to be brutally persecuted behind the barbed wire fences of North Korea's political prison camps, subjected to unrelenting induced malnutrition, forced labor, torture, sexual violence as well as public and secret executions. Those suspected of being disloyal to the regime, of being, from the regime's viewpoint, *wrong-thinkers, wrong-doers,* of possessing *wrong knowledge,* of having engaged in *wrong associations,* or of coming from the *wrong family background,* are subjected to extrajudicial arrest and detention, often together with members of three generations of their families. They are held in North Korea's *hidden gulag* indefinitely, in most cases without charge or hope for recourse.

In the year 2014, pursuant to *Songbun*— a system of social discrimination established in the 1950s—the people of North Korea continue to be divided into three social categories and 51 subcategories, based on their degree of loyalty to the regime, and on the perceived allegiance of their parents and grandparents. Their access to food, jobs, and any type of opportunity continues to depend on their social classification. In the mid to late 1990s, as up to 3 million North Koreans starved to death, the Kim regime continued to invest in the development of its ballistic missile and nuclear weapons programs, and purchased 30 MiG-29 fighters from Belarus and Russia, and 40 MiG-21 fighters from Kazakhstan.

Human Rights Trends under the Kim Jong-un Regime

The human rights situation has deteriorated under the Kim Jong-un regime. Three trends stand out in particular: an aggressive crackdown on attempted defections—the number of North Korean escapees arriving in South Korea declined by almost 50% from 2011 to 2012/2013); an aggressive purge—culminating in the execution of Jang Sung-taek, the leader's uncle, and his associates in December 2013; and the "restructuring" of North Korea's political prison camp system—facilities near the border with China have been closed, while other camps have been expanded.

The UN Commission of Inquiry (COI)

On March 21, 2013, the United Nations Human Rights Council—composed of 47 UN member states—adopted *by consensus* a resolution to establish a "Commission of Inquiry on Human Rights in the Democratic People's Republic of Korea (COI)." While NGOs such as HRNK, tasked to monitor, research and report on the North Korean human rights situation, had been aware of the extent of the North Korean human rights violations for many years, this was the first time that an investigative body was established by the United Nations to determine the extent and gravity of North Korea's human rights abuses.

After investigating "the systematic, widespread and grave violations of human rights" in North Korea, the COI released its draft report on February 17, one month ahead of the formal submission to the UN Human Rights Council on March 17. The report finds that "in many instances, the violations found entailed crimes against humanity based on State policies."[1]

---

[1] Human Rights Council, A.HRC.25.63, *Report of the commission of inquiry on human rights in the Democratic Republic of Korea,* February 17, 2014, http://www.ohchr.org/EN/HRBodies/HRC/CoIDPRK/Pages/ReportoftheCommissionofInquiryDPRK.aspx.

The COI's Findings

The COI has determined that systematic, widespread and gross human rights violations have been, and are being, committed by North Korea. These include:
- arbitrary detention, torture, executions and enforced disappearance to political prison camps;
- violations of the freedoms of thought, expression and religion;
- discrimination on the basis of State-assigned social class, gender, and disability
- violations of the freedom of movement and residence, including the right to leave one's own country;
- violations of the right to food and related aspects of the right to life ; and
- enforced disappearance of persons from other countries, including through international abductions.

In light of the gravity, scale and level of organization of these violations, the COI has concluded that crimes against humanity have been committed by officials of the Democratic People's Republic of Korea, pursuant to policies established at the highest level of the State. These crimes against humanity involve extermination, murder, enslavement, torture, imprisonment, rape, forced abortions and other sexual violence, persecution on political, religious, racial and gender grounds, the forcible transfer of populations, the enforced disappearance of persons and the inhumane act of knowingly causing prolonged starvation. The COI has also established that crimes against humanity continue to be committed in North Korea because the policies, institutions and patterns of impunity that lie at their heart remain in place.

One of the most important determinations made by the COI is that North Korea can be characterized as a totalitarian state that does not content itself with ensuring the authoritarian rule of a small group of people, but seeks to dominate every aspect of its citizens' lives and terrorizes them from within. In other words, the COI has found that crimes against humanity and other abysmal human rights violations are at the very core of the North Korean regime's *modus operandi*. The COI has characterized North Korea as "a state that does not have any parallel in the contemporary world," due to the "gravity, scale, and nature of the violations committed" by the North Korean regime.

The Victims of North Korea's Crimes against Humanity

The COI determined that crimes against humanity target anyone viewed as a threat to the political system and leadership of North Korea, in particular:
- the estimated 80,000-120,000 inmates of the DPRK's political prison camps;
- inmates of other detention facilities, including political prisoners;
- persons who try to escape North Korea, in particular those forcibly repatriated by China to conditions of danger;
- religious believers, Christians in particular;

- people considered to introduce "subversive" influences into North Korea, such as those who smuggle South Korean video material into North Korea, or those who are suspected of having had contacts with South Koreans;
- the COI determined that crimes against humanity have been committed by deliberately starving selected segments of the North Korean population, in particular during the great famine of the 1990s. The purpose of *de facto* condemning targeted groups to death by starvation was the preservation of North Korea's leadership and political system;
- the COI found that crimes against humanity have been, and are being committed against the citizens of the Republic of Korea, Japan, and other countries abducted by agents of the North Korean regime.

What Actions Should Be Taken by the United States and International Community to Hold North Korea Accountable?

The COI has emphasized that the international community has the responsibility to protect the population of North Korea from further crimes against humanity, as their own State distinctly fails to do so. The COI has recommended a multi-faceted approach to implement this responsibility to protect, by combining urgent accountability measures with a reinforced human rights dialogue. The COI pointed out that, since the government of North Korea is not willing to prosecute its own officials, the United Nations will have to ensure that those most responsible for crimes against humanity are held accountable. The COI further recommended that *the UN Security Council refer the North Korean situation to the International Criminal Court.* The European Union, together with Japan, Australia, and South Korea clearly stated their support for Security Council referral to the International Criminal Court on March 17, following the formal submission of the COI report to the UN Human Rights Council.

The COI further recommended that the UN High Commissioner for Human Rights establish a field-based presence in the region to document human rights violations in the DPRK, in particular where they amount to crimes against humanity, in order to continue to focus attention on the human rights situation in that country.

Due in particular to potential opposition by the People's Republic of China, a permanent member of the UN Security Council, the referral of the North Korean case by the UN Security Council to the International Criminal Court is unlikely, at least over the short term. However, it can be argued that, by bringing the case to the UN Security Council and thus forcing a Chinese veto, the spotlight will be on China, which continues to unconditionally extend its support and protection to the Kim regime, and to refuse North Korean escapees access to the process leading to their acquiring political refugee status. In a letter dated December 16, 2013, the COI has already urged the Government of the People's Republic of China to warn relevant officials that the forcible repatriation of North Korean refugees to conditions of extreme danger—involving persecution, torture, prolonged arbitrary detention, sexual violence, forced abortions, and infanticide—could amount to the aiding and abetting of crimes against humanity.

For more than two decades, the United States and the international community have been concerned with the grave political security challenges posed by the North Korean regime. Concern for North Korea's egregious human rights violations hasn't been similarly reflected in either the sanctions regime imposed on North Korea or attempts to engage in bilateral or multilateral dialogue. The *inclusion of North Korean human rights in the UN Security Council's permanent agenda* would be a long overdue and feasible measure, since 9 out of 15 votes of permanent and non-permanent members of the Council would be needed, and such course of action could not be blocked by the veto of a permanent member.

In order to create an atmosphere conducive—at the very least—to the inclusion of North Korean human rights in the UN Security Council's permanent agenda, over the short term, considering *the application of the Arria Formula* could be an effective approach to be pursued by the United States and like-minded Council members. The Arria Formula is an informal arrangement ensuring that the Council has greater flexibility in its ability to be briefed on international peace and security issues. The formula also allows members of the Council to invite speakers other than UN officials, delegations or high-ranking officials of Council members.

While recognizing that the report by the COI is a critical and historic step by the United Nations, HRNK also urges the United States Government to **support greater involvement by UN agencies in North Korea, beyond the human rights bodies.** HRNK insists that UN agencies to which the United States Government is a significant contributor, agencies tasked with development or humanitarian assistance—including UNICEF, WHO, WFP and UNFPA—should be fully aware of the findings of the UN Commission of Inquiry and find ways to promote them.

HRNK urges the United States Government to *extend its support to NGOs and other organizations tasked to monitor and report on North Korea's human rights violations.* In particular, efforts to document crimes against humanity in North Korea and to identify those responsible will be critical to efforts to ensure accountability as well as preparations for a future effective transitional justice program in North Korea.

Should the COI Report Provoke Changes to the U.S. "Strategic Patience" Policy?

U.S. North Korea policy has been dominated by grave political security concerns, including North Korea's development of its ballistic missile and nuclear weapons program, and also serious military provocations, such as the sinking of the ROKS Cheonan in March 2010, or the shelling of South Korea's Yeonpyeong Island in November of the same year. The policy of "strategic patience"—implying that the United States can afford to wait for North Korea's decision to denuclearize, or for a set of circumstances conducive to North Korean denuclearization—appears to make sense within a context defined by the North Korean regime's established patterns of behavior, involving the alternation of provocations and "charm offensives."

From the *Treaty on the Non-Proliferation of Nuclear Weapons (NPT)* and the *1994 Geneva Agreed Framework* and the *Six Party Talks* to the February 2012 *Leap Day Agreement*, the North Korean regime has rescinded each and every commitment it has made, in multilateral or bilateral talks. The North Korean regime's utter lack of international credibility suggests that "strategic patience" is one of very few options left to the U.S. Government. Moreover, the historic record of the past two decades denotes that the assumption that North Korea continues to develop its nuclear and missile capabilities unless the United States initiates bilateral or multilateral dialogue is flawed. The North Korean regime continues such developments regardless of the status of bilateral or multilateral talks, with the ultimate goal of miniaturizing a nuclear warhead to the point where it can be mounted on a long-range ballistic missile capable of reaching the continental United States. From the viewpoint of the North Korean regime, such development is essential to its survival, and to North Korea's maintaining international relevance.

Nonetheless, the COI report has confirmed what human rights NGOs and research organizations had known for years: crimes against humanity have been, and are being committed in North Korea. Under the regime of Kim Jong-un, as many as 23,000 political prisoners disappeared prior to the transfer of the prison population from Camp No. 22 in Hoeryong, North Hamgyeong Province, to other detention facilities.[2] As the horror of what author Mark Helprin termed a "slow-motion holocaust" continues, the people and government of the United States can unambiguously afford no "strategic patience" that would allow the Kim regime more time to abuse, starve, wrongfully imprison, maim, torture, and kill the innocent men, women, and children of North Korea.

Human rights are at the very core of the fundamental values that define us, values that Americans share with our friends, allies, and partners in the Asia-Pacific region and beyond, first and foremost with the Republic of Korea. Recent developments in the Middle East confirm that tyrants who violate the rights of their own citizens with impunity become threats to regional and international peace and security, especially if they are armed with weapons of mass destruction. Consequently, rather than applying "strategic patience" to the U.S. approach to the human rights crisis in North Korea, or postponing significant policy measures until the circumstances have changed, *the United States must include human rights in the North Korea policy agenda.* The next requisite steps should comprise *the inclusion of human rights concerns in the agenda of future bilateral and multilateral talks* and *linking the international sanctions regime to the human rights situation in North Korea.*

How Could Effective and Targeted Sanctions against the North Korean Regime Improve Its Human Rights Situation?

The international sanctions regime against North Korea, established through UN Security Council Resolutions 825, 1540, 1695, 1718, 1874, 2087, and 2094, aims to prevent the development and proliferation of weapons of mass destruction and ballistic missile

---

[2] Hawk, David. *North Korea's Hidden Gulag: Interpreting Reports of Changes in the Prison Camps,* page 22. Committee for Human Rights in North Korea, 2013.

technology by North Korea. The current international sanctions regime is not linked to North Korea's human rights situation. In order to achieve international momentum and a degree of effectiveness comparable to that applied to efforts to do away with South Africa's apartheid, *the international sanctions regime must be expanded beyond counter-proliferation efforts, and be linked to North Korea's human rights situation.*

The COI has determined that the main perpetrators of human rights violations and crimes against humanity are officials of North Korea's State Security Department (SSD, the Ministry of People's Security (MSC), the Korean People's Army (KPA), the Office of the Public Prosecutor, the judiciary and the Korean Workers' Party (KWP). These officials have been acting under the effective control of the leadership organs of the KWP, the National Defense Commission (NDC) and the leader of North Korea. A sanctions regime effectively addressing the North Korean human rights situation must *sever access to funds aimed to support, aid and abet the crimes against humanity and other human rights violations* perpetrated by the North Korean regime, until the situation has been verifiably remedied (i.e. the political prison camps have been closed, full disclosure has been brought to the issue of abductions of foreign nationals etc.). Effective sanctions would also *sever the access to luxury goods and foreign travel for those officials most responsible for North Korea's crimes against humanity.*

On more than one occasion, HRNK has called upon the international community to concern itself not only with security and nuclear issues, but with the persecution, starvation and political repression of the North Korean population. The COI recommended that the UN Security Council impose targeted individual sanctions against those most responsible for North Korea's systematic, widespread and gross human rights violations, and crimes against humanity. The COI further recommended that states should not use the provision of food and other essential humanitarian assistance to impose pressure on North Korea, and that humanitarian assistance should be provided in accordance with humanitarian and human rights principles, including the principle of non-discrimination, while the North Korean authorities should provide adequate conditions of humanitarian access and related monitoring.

Following the letter and spirit of the COI report, effective targeted sanctions aiming to improve the human rights situation in North Korea would ensure that adequately monitored humanitarian assistance reaches those who need it most, in particular the most vulnerable people of North Korea. While targeting the perpetrators of crimes against humanity, effective sanctions regimes must ensure that funds that would otherwise have been spent on ski lifts, luxury goods, and weapons be used to purchase food, medicine, and other humanitarian supplies for the people of North Korea.

Mr. CHABOT. Thank you. We appreciate your testimony. Mr. Klingner, you're recognized for 5 minutes.

STATEMENT OF MR. BRUCE KLINGNER, SENIOR RESEARCH FELLOW, NORTHEAST ASIA, THE HERITAGE FOUNDATION

Mr. KLINGNER. Thank you, Mr. Chairman and distinguished members of the panel. It is truly an honor to be asked to appear before you on such an important issue to our national security.

As we've heard from my colleagues, North Korea's crimes against humanity clearly show the regime is a threat to its citizens. North Korea under Kim Jong-un has also demonstrated it is a military threat to U.S. allies in Asia, a worldwide proliferation threat, and increasingly a direct military threat to the United States.

It is fitting that today's hearing occurs on the 4-year anniversary of North Korea's sinking of the South Korean naval ship, Cheonan, a North Korean act of war which resulted in the deaths of 46 South Korean sailors.

North Korea has made greater progress than widely perceived—if not already achieved—warhead miniaturization, the ability to place nuclear weapons on its short-range missiles, and a preliminary ability to reach the United States. As such, the United States and its allies face a greater threat today than is widely construed.

Despite repeated U.S. attempts at diplomacy, North Korea refuses to abide by the commitments it made during numerous international agreements to give up the nuclear weapons that it had previously agreed never to pursue in the first place. North Korea now demands recognition as a nuclear armed state. It declared, ''There will be no more discussions over denuclearization of the Korean Peninsula,'' and proclaimed, ''Only fools will entertain the delusion that we will trade our nuclear deterrent for petty economic aid.''

Despite initial hopes that the new Chinese leadership would more fully implement U.N.-required actions against North Korea, Beijing instead continues to be part of the problem rather than part of the solution. Clearly, the United States cannot rely on China to constrain North Korea.

President Obama declared that North Korea's nuclear weapons program was a ''threat to U.S. national security'' and vowed ''significant, serious enforcement of sanctions,'' but despite this, the United States has pursued a policy in which we only incrementally increase punishments on Pyongyang toward repeated defiance of the international community.

The United States has pulled its punches when targeting financial measures against North Korea. By contrast, the U.S., EU, and U.N. have imposed far more pervasive and compelling measures against Iran, even though Pyongyang and not Tehran has withdrawn from the non-proliferation treaty, tested nuclear weapons, and repeatedly threatened nuclear attacks on the United States and its allies.

By adopting a sanctions policy of timid incrementalism, with promises to be tougher the next time that North Korea misbehaves, the U.S. is squandering the opportunity to more effectively impede progress on North Korea's nuclear and missile programs, and coerce compliance with U.N. resolutions. Just as strong measures induced Iran back to the negotiating table, more robust sanctions are needed to leverage North Korea.

There is a widespread misperception that North Korea is the most heavily sanctioned country in the world, and there's nothing more that can be done. That is simply not true. In my submitted testimony I've provided an extensive list of additional specific financial measures that the U.S. can and should impose on North Korea, as well as against non-North Korean entities that are violating U.S. law and U.N. resolutions.

Most of these recommended actions have already been applied against other nations, including Iran and Burma. These are targeted financial measures against the regime and other violators, not the North Korean people themselves. In essence, they are financial precision guided munitions and not economic carpet bombing against the populace.

Since it is a unilateral U.S. financial strategy against violators, China cannot veto it and Beijing will find it harder to block than a diplomatic strategy or traditional trade sanctions.

A few of these recommended actions are to: Designate North Korea as a primary money laundering concern, as the U.S. previously did with Iran and Burma; ban North Korean financial institutions correspondent accounts in the United States—even financial institutions not doing business in the U.S. would be affected since nearly all dollar denominated transactions internationally must pass through U.S. Treasury-regulated banks; publicly identify and sanction all foreign companies, financial institutions, and governments assisting North Korea's nuclear and missile programs; impose third-party sanctions on entities that trade with those on a sanctions list; compel the removal of North Korea from the SWIFT financial transfer network as Iranian banks were in 2012; formally charge North Korea as a currency counterfeiter; tighten maritime counter proliferation by targeting shipping companies and airlines caught proliferating; and finally, enhance U.S. inspections of shipping companies transiting ports that consistently fail to inspect North Korean cargo.

In conclusion, the current U.S. policy of Strategic Patience is predominantly passive because it fails to impose sufficient pressure to effectively degrade North Korea's capabilities or alter its behavior. Minimalist measures have only encouraged North Korea to continue to expand and refine its nuclear arsenal of missiles and embolden it to proliferate. The U.S. has sufficient tools, it has only lacked the resolve to use them.

Finally, I would submit that the operative question should be why would the United States hesitate to impose the same measures on North Korea that Washington has already implemented on other countries for far less egregious violations?

I thank you again for the opportunity to appear before you, and I look forward to your questions.

[The prepared statement of Mr. Klingner follows:]

The Heritage Foundation

LEADERSHIP FOR AMERICA

214 Massachusetts Avenue, NE • Washington DC 20002 • (202) 546-4400 • heritage.org

CONGRESSIONAL TESTIMONY

Going Beyond 'Strategic Patience:' Time to Get North Korean Sanctions Right

Testimony before
Asia Subcommittee of the Foreign Affairs Committee
United States House of Representatives

"The Shocking Truth about North Korean Tyranny"

March 26, 2014

Bruce Klingner
Senior Research Fellow, Northeast Asia
The Heritage Foundation

My name is Bruce Klingner. I am the Senior Research Fellow for Northeast Asia at The Heritage Foundation. The views I express in this testimony are my own, and should not be construed as representing any official position of The Heritage Foundation.

Assessing North Korea's Nuclear and Missile Threat
Experts predominantly assert that North Korea has developed several nuclear devices but not yet mastered the ability to miniaturize the warhead nor deliver it via missile. Media reports habitually declare that North Korean missiles cannot yet reach the United States.

Based on this benign conclusion, policymakers presume the United States and its allies still have several years to diplomatically constrain North Korea's nuclear program, pursue timidly incremental sanctions, and prepare military defenses.

However, this analytic construct is flawed since it, for example, gives insufficient weight to Pyongyang's lengthy collaborative nuclear and missile relationship with Pakistan, a country that all experts assess already has nuclear weapons deliverable by missile. North Korean scientists provided critical assistance to Islamabad's missile programs in return for reciprocal uranium-based nuclear weapon expertise, technology, and components.

Moreover, analysts have frequently underestimated North Korea's nuclear and missile programs due to ideologically-driven analysis, political expediency, and the belief that a technically backward nation could not have achieved the necessary breakthroughs. The potential for continued regime refinement of its nuclear and missile arsenal was often discounted until confronted with irrefutable evidence.

Skeptics initially dismissed evidence of North Korea's plutonium-based nuclear weapons, its highly enriched uranium program, involvement in constructing a Syrian nuclear reactor, and ability to develop long-range missiles. U.S. intelligence estimates of these programs were dismissed as politically motivated, until they were proven unquestioningly correct.

North Korea has likely made greater progress than perceived -- if not already achieved -- warhead miniaturization, the ability to place nuclear weapons on its short range missiles, and a preliminary ability to reach the United States. As such, the United States and its allies face a greater threat today than is widely construed.

Nuclear programs. Pyongyang began its plutonium-based nuclear weapons program in the 1960s and now likely has 6-10 nuclear weapons. Even as Pyongyang signed several agreements to never pursue a nuclear weapons program, it began in the late 1980s to develop a second, parallel path to acquiring nuclear weapons using uranium.

A.Q. Khan, the father of Pakistan's nuclear weapons program, provided a nuclear package deal to Pyongyang including warhead designs, centrifuges, and nuclear fuel.[1] The warhead design may have been the same he provided to Libya which contained

---

[1] David Sanger, "U.S. Sees More Arms Ties Between Pakistan and Korea," The New York Times, March 14, 2004.

detailed, step by step instructions to produce a Chinese-designed nuclear warhead that would be deliverable by North Korea's No Dong missile.[2]

Pakistan assistance increased dramatically in 1997 when Islamabad began paying for North Korean missiles by sharing nuclear weapons secrets. According to a CIA National Intelligence Estimate, Pakistan provided information to North Korea on building and testing uranium-based nuclear weapons and helped Pyongyang conduct a series of "cold tests," simulated nuclear explosions, using uranium. Pakistan also provided advice on how to hide nuclear research from American satellites.[3]

In 2010, Pyongyang disclosed the uranium program by displaying 2,000 centrifuges to a visiting U.S. scientist who was stunned by the scope and sophistication of the program which exceeded all expert predictions. North Korea likely has additional covert uranium enrichment facilities and has sought enough components for at least 10,000 centrifuges.[4]

It is suspected but not proven that the February 2013 nuclear test was of a uranium-based weapon. If so, then Pyongyang has a break-out capability to augment its nuclear arsenal. In November 2013, South Korean Minister of Defense Kim Kwan-jin testified that North Korea has the ability to build uranium-based nuclear weapons.[5]

Missiles. North Korea began developing missiles in the late 1970s by reverse-engineering Soviet-designed Scud-B missiles acquired from Egypt. Pyongyang extrapolated this technology to build extended-range Scuds, No Dong missiles, and the Taepo Dong ICBM.

North Korea exported No Dong missiles to Iran and Pakistan, providing the basis for those countries' Shehab and Ghauri missiles. The initial Iranian and Pakistan missiles displayed in military parades were manufactured solely in North Korea. In 1992, North Korea signed an agreement for Tehran to provide $500 million for joint development of nuclear weapons and No Dong ballistic missiles."[6]

A.Q. Khan described how, in return for Pakistani assistance to Pyongyang's centrifuge program, *"North Korea would help Pakistan in fitting the nuclear warhead into the Ghauri missile."*[7] Khan's assertion is important since analysts continue to assert that North Korea has not yet developed the ability to mount nuclear warheads on its No Dong missile while unequivocally accepting Pakistan has done so.

---

[2] Joby Warrick and Peter Slevin, "Libyan Arms Designs Traced Back to China," Washington Post, February 15, 2004.

[3] Seymour Hersh. "The Cold Test." The New Yorker, January 27, 2003.

[4] David Albright, "North Korea's Estimated Stocks of Plutonium and Weapon-Grade Uranium. ISIS.

[5] Kim Eun-jung, "N. Korea can produce uranium-based nuclear bomb: Seoul's defense chief," Yonhap, November 20, 2013.

[6] Daniel Pinkston, "The North Korean Ballistic Missile Program," Strategic Studies Institute, February 2008, p. 18.

[7] R. Jeffrey Smith and Joby Warrick, "Pakistani scientist depicts more advanced nuclear program in North Korea," The Washington Post, December 28, 2009.

North Korea currently has an extensive ballistic missile force. Pyongyang has deployed approximately 800 Scud short-range tactical ballistic missiles, 300 No Dong medium-range missiles, and 50 Musudan intermediate-range ballistic missiles. The Scud missiles threaten South Korea, the No Dong can target all of Japan, while the Musudan can hit U.S. bases on Okinawa and Guam. Pyongyang continues development of the Taepo Dong series of intercontinental ballistic missiles.[8]

North Korea claims nuclear capable missiles. North Korea now asserts it is fully nuclear strike capability. In October 2012, the National Defense Commission warned its strategic rocket forces can hit U.S. bases in South Korea, Japan, and Guam as well as the U.S. mainland.[9] North Korea announced in February 2013 that its nuclear test was a "miniaturized and lighter" nuclear weapon that could be fit atop a missile[10]

In March 2013, the Korea People's Army Supreme Command warned that "The U.S. should not forget that Anderson AFB in Guam [and] naval bases in Japan and Okinawa are within striking range of the DPRK's precision strike means."[11] Pyongyang threatened to turn Seoul and Washington into "seas of fire" through a "diversified precise nuclear strike,"[12] using "lighter and smaller nukes unlike what they had in the past."[13] 'Diversified' was interpreted as Pyongyang having developing both plutonium and uranium weapons.

US. and allies increasingly assess North Korea is nuclear capable. After recovering components of the North Korean long-range missile launched in December 2012, South Korea assessed it had "a range of more than 10,000 kilometers."[14] In March 2013, Minister of Defense Kim Kwan-jin told the National Assembly that the missile could have reached the U.S. west coast.[15]

U.S. Vice Chairman of the Joint Chiefs of Staff James Winnefeld stated in March 2013, "We believe the KN-08 probably does have the range to reach the United States. The North Korean threat went just a little bit faster than we might have expected."[16] In April

---

[8] "North Korea's Nuclear and Missile Programs," International Crisis Group. June 18, 2009, http://www.crisisgroup.org/~/media/Files/asia/north-east-asia/north-korea/168_north_koreas_nuclear_and_missile_programs.ashx.

[9] "North Korea Says Its Rockets Could Hit Continental US," Chosun Ilbo, October 12, 2012.

[10] Note verbale from the Permanent Mission of the Democratic People's Republic of Korea to the United Nations addressed to the President of the Security Council. February 13, 2013, http://www.undocs.org/S/2013/91

[11] "North Korea says U.S. bases in Japan, Guam could be targeted by nukes," Mainichi Shimbun, March 21, 2013.

[12] Choe Sang-hyun, "North Korea Threatens to Attack U.S. With 'Lighter and Smaller Nukes'," The New York Times, March 5, 2013.

[13] Choe Sang-hun, North Korea Threatens to Attack U.S. With 'Lighter and Smaller Nukes', New York Times, March 5, 2013, http://www.nytimes.com/2013/03/06/world/asia/north-korea-threatens-to-attack-us-with-lighter-and-smaller-nukes.html.

[14] "S. Korea Says Debris Reveals North's ICBM Technology," Voice of America, December 23, 2012.

[15] "N. Korea Rocket Could Fly 10,000km," Chosun Ilbo, April 16, 2012

[16] Park Hyun, "US to boost missile defense in response to North Korean threats," Hankyoreh, March 18, 2013.

2013, the Obama Administration reversed its previous decision to cut construction of 14 additional missile defense interceptors in Alaska claiming an unexpected, sudden acceleration of the North Korean missile threat.

U.S. experts privately commented that the recovered North Korean missile provided "tangible proof that North Korea was building the missile's cone at dimensions for a nuclear warhead, durable enough to be placed on a long-range missile that could re-enter the earth's atmosphere from space." A U.S. official added that South Korea also provided other intelligence that suggested North Korea had "mastered the miniaturization and warhead design as well."[17]

In April 2013, U.S. officials told reporters that North Korea "can put a nuclear weapon on a missile, that they have missile-deliverable nuclear nukes, but not ones that can go more than 1,000 miles."[18]

In March 2014, General Charles Jacoby, chief of the North American Aerospace Defense Command, testified that "tangible evidence of North Korean and Iranian ambitions reinforces our understanding of how the ballistic missile threat to the homeland has matured from a theoretical to a practical consideration."[19]

Battle for power, not policy in Pyongyang
Despite some initial naive predictions that Kim Jong-UN would be a reformer, there were unmistakable signals from the beginning that he would not deviate from existing policies. Real economic reform requires a willingness to incorporate foreign capitalist precepts into North Korea's socialist system. But doing so would entail opening North Korea to the outside world.

Kim Jong-un instead unequivocally affirmed the continuation of North Korea's centrally-planned socialist economy. Frustrated by frequent foreign speculation of North Korea reform, Pyongyang even denounced such suggestions as "the height of ignorance. To expect policy change and reform and opening from [North Korea] is nothing but a foolish and silly dream…There cannot be any slightest change in all policies."[20]

Pyongyang's diktat on the unitary leadership of Kim Jong-un does not broach any resistance. If there was doubt that Kim Jong-un would be just as merciless as his father and grandfather, it died along with Jang Song-taek.

Kim has emulated the power politics of his father and grandfather but taken it to new levels of brutality. During his two years in power, Kim Jong-un has unleashed the

[17] Eli Lake, "US Recovery of North Korean satellite exposed nuclear progress," The Daily Beast, April 15, 2013.
[18] Richard Engel, "Will North Korea follow through on nuclear threats?," NBC Nightly News, April 3, 2013, http://www.nbcnews.com/video/nightly-news/51421978#51421978.
[19] Statement of General Charles H. Jacoby, Jr., Commander United States Northern Command and North American Aerospace Defense Command before the Senate Armed Services Committee, March 13, 2014, http://www.armed-services.senate.gov/imo/media/doc/Jacoby_03-13-14.pdf.
[20] "North Korea dismisses South's talk of reform." BBC. July 29, 2012.

security services to eliminate enemies within the government and escalated the subjugation of the populace. He increased public executions, expanded the gulags for political prisoners, and increased government punishment for people caught with information from the outside world to intimidate the populace. Kim had 80 people executed simply for watching foreign videos.[21]

Do purges reflect stability or instability?

Korea watchers are debating whether Jang's purge reflects a weak or strong North Korean leader. Some experts perceive an embattled Kim Jong-un desperately fending off real or imagined challengers. But it is more likely that the purge of hundreds of North Korean officials since 2011 shows Kim is firmly in control and confident enough to remove even the senior most officials.

Regime change in the foreseeable future is unlikely due to the pervasiveness of North Korean security services, the lack of a viable opposition party or movement, and the state's absolute control over information sources. Moreover, China and South Korea – fearful of the consequences of a collapsing regime – have often increased aid and developmental assistance when economic collapse appeared imminent.

To be sure, a stable North Korea does not equate to a non-threatening North Korea. Kim Jong-un has shown himself to be just as belligerent and dangerous as his predecessors. Indeed, he raised tensions to perilously high levels in early 2013, with strategic and tactical threats against the United States, South Korea, and Japan.

Kim Jong-un has maintained Kim Jong-il's foreign policy but appears to be implementing it a more volatile, reckless, and unpredictable manner. Indeed, it appears Jong-un may not have a game plan.

Kim's refusal to implement economic reform dooms his country's economy to continued abysmal conditions. His threatening antics have poisoned the well for North Korea to receive the level of foreign resources and benefits necessary to improve the national economy. Unable to achieve its economic and diplomatic objectives, North Korea will return to provocations and threats.

The North Korean threat -- always high -- has gotten worse under the young leader. There can be debate as to how best to address the situation. But there should be no debate as to just how dangerous the situation could become.

North Korean Commits Crimes Against Humanity

The United Nations Commission of Inquiry report provides a chilling litany of horrors that the North Korean regime has inflicted upon its citizens. Based upon overwhelming evidence, the commission issued a damning condemnation of the North Korea government for "systemic, widespread, and gross violations of human rights."

---

[21] Julian Ryall, North Korea executes 80 people for watch foreign films," The Sydney Morning Herald, November 13, 2013.

The commission concluded that these human rights abuses were of such a monumental scale as to constitute crimes against humanity. The panel recommended the U.N. Security Council refer the situation to the International Criminal Court or the establishment of an ad hoc U.N. tribunal for prosecution. The commission also advocated adopting targeted sanctions against those most responsible for these crimes against humanity

Beijing characteristically dismissed the report as "divorced from reality" and vowed it would block any further action against North Korea. China's foreign ministry spokesperson declared "Submitting this report to the ICC will not help resolve the human rights situation in the relevant country."

The Shame of Inaction. The commission underscored how North Korea's decades-long perpetration of "crimes that shock the conscience of humanity raises questions about the inadequacy of the response of the international community. The international community must accept its responsibility to protect the people of the Democratic People's Republic of Korea from crimes against humanity."

Commission Chairman Michael Kirby eloquently implored, "Now is a time for action. We can't say we didn't know. The suffering and tears of the people of North Korea demand action."

There should be widespread international outrage against the horrors systemically perpetuated on the North Korean people by their leaders. North Korea's killing fields must disappear. Time is running out for the North Korean people, but too many have already perished as the world turned its back."

What Should Be Done
The U.S. should:
- Examine existing human rights legislation to ensure that penalties imposed on North Korea are consistent with those enacted against other human rights violators.
- Impose targeted financial measures against all North Korean entities—and their leadership—identified by the commission and then call upon other nations to take commensurate action.
- Publicly highlight not only Chinese obstructionism to addressing North Korea's heinous human rights abuses but also, as delineated in the commission report, Chinese complicity. For example, Beijing's forced repatriation of refugees are in violation of several international accords.
- Urge South Korea to pass its first North Korean Human Rights Act, which would provide funding for human rights groups and impose conditions on engagement with Pyongyang. Since its first introduction in 2005, the progressive South Korean Democratic Party has resisted approving legislation or even criticizing North Korean human rights violations.

Timid U.S. Responses to North Korean Threat

Responding to North Korea's third nuclear test in 2013, President Barack Obama declared that North Korea's nuclear weapons program was a "threat to the U.S. national security and to international peace and security."[22] The U.N. Security Council similarly warned that North Korea's nuclear and missile threats posed "a clear threat to international peace and security."[23] In 2009, Obama had vowed that North Korean "belligerent, provocative behavior that threatens neighbors will be met with significant, serious enforcement of sanctions."[24]

Yet despite these unambiguous warnings and unequivocal vows of resolute response, the United States continues to implement timid policies that only incrementally increase punishments on Pyongyang for its repeated defiance of the international community. The United States still pulls its punches when targeting financial measures against North Korea and its supporting entities, and the U.S. has shied away from effective unilateral action since 2006. By contrast, the U.S. has led the charge for far more pervasive and compelling measures against Iran, despite Tehran's greater diplomatic and economic interaction with the rest of the world.

The United States should use its action against Iran as a model and impose the same severity of targeted financial measures against North Korea. While there are mitigating factors, North Korea's limited nodes of economic contact with the outside world and lack of a valuable global commodity—such as Iran's oil—make it vulnerable to enhanced economic pressure.

Sanctions: An Important and Variable Component of Foreign Policy
Sanctions[25] are punitive measures intended to deter, coerce, and compel changes in another country's policy and behavior. During the past decade, the U.S. government adopted a more effective financial strategy against rogue regimes. Washington now uses *targeted* financial measures against regimes and violators and not the citizens of a country. In essence, these are economic precision-guided missiles rather than indiscriminate economic carpet bombing.

This new strategy is based on several key precepts:
1. Even the most isolated regime has to move its money across borders;
2. Because the U.S. dollar is the principal reserve and trading currency around the world, almost all international transactions are denominated in dollars which must go through the U.S. financial system;

[22] Calum MacLeod and Sunny Yang, "U.N. Condemns North Korea Nuclear Test, Promises Action," *USA Today*, February 12, 2013, http://www.usatoday.com/story/news/world/2013/02/11/earthquake-north-korea-nuclear-test/1911587/.

[23] U.N. Security Council, Resolution 2094, S/RES/2094 (2013). March 7, 2013. http://www.un.org/en/ga/search/view_doc.asp?symbol=S/RES/2094(2013).

[24] Barack Obama and Lee Myung-Bak, "Remarks by President Obama and President Lee Myung-Bak of the Republic of Korea in Joint Press Availability," June 16, 2009, http://www.whitehouse.gov/the-press-office/remarks-president-obama-and-president-lee-republic-korea-joint-press-availability.

[25] For the purposes of this paper, the terms *sanctions, targeted financial or regulatory measures,* and *coercive financial pressure* will be used interchangeably, although there are some technical differences among them.

3. Financial institutions are driven to police themselves by aversion to reputational risk and exclusion from the U.S. financial system, which provides Washington with very strong leverage against rogue regimes.

The debate over the utility of financial pressure in foreign policy is usually depicted in binary fashion, such as whether the U.S. should use sanctions or engagement.

The reality, of course, is that sanctions and engagement—along with economic assistance, military deterrence, alliances, and public diplomacy—are diplomatic tools to influence the behavior of other nations. These tools can be employed in a range of options and combinations.

Rather than being used in isolation, sanctions and engagement are most effective when integrated into a comprehensive strategy that engages all of the instruments of national power. Not fully utilizing any element of national power reduces the effectiveness of U.S. foreign policy.

Critics of coercive financial pressure question its effectiveness because they have not yet forced Pyongyang to abandon its nuclear and missile programs, but neither did repeated bilateral and multilateral negotiations or unconditional engagement. Adopting such a narrow viewpoint overlooks the multifaceted utility of sanctions, which:

1. Show resolve to enforce international agreements and send a strong signal to other nuclear aspirants. If laws are not enforced and defended, they cease to have value.
2. Impose a heavy penalty on violators to demonstrate that there are consequences for defying international agreements and transgressing the law.
3. Constrain North Korea's ability to acquire the components, technology, and finances to augment and expand its arsenal.
4. Impede North Korean nuclear, missile, and conventional arms proliferation. Targeted financial and regulatory measures increase both the risk and the operating costs of North Korea's continued violations of Security Council resolutions and international law.
5. In conjunction with other policy tools, seek to modify North Korean behavior.

The U.N. Security Council established a Panel of Experts to review member countries' implementation of Security Council resolutions imposed on North Korea. In June 2013, the panel concluded:

[W]hile the imposition of sanctions has not halted the development of nuclear and ballistic missile programs, it has in all likelihood considerably delayed the [North Korean] timetable and ...choked off significant funding which would have been channeled into its prohibited activities. [It] has hampered its arms sales and illicit weapon programs. The resolutions are also crucial in preventing the country from exporting sensitive nuclear and missile technology.[26]

Tougher Sanctions on Iran Than on North Korea
North Korea has withdrawn from the Non-Proliferation Treaty, developed and tested nuclear weapons, declared that its nuclear program is for military purposes, and threatened the United States and its allies with nuclear annihilation. As great a threat as Iran's nuclear program is, Tehran has done none of these things. Yet the U.S., the European Union, and the United Nations have imposed far less restrictive sanctions against Pyongyang than against Tehran.

Iran. For decades, the United States has imposed sanctions on Iran for a variety of transgressions. President Jimmy Carter barred U.S. purchase of Iranian oil in response to Iran's taking U.S. diplomatic hostages in 1979. The sanctions were subsequently removed but then reimposed by President Ronald Reagan in 1987 because of Iran's "active support of terrorism" and "aggressive and unlawful action against U.S. flag vessels … in the international waters of the Persian Gulf."[27]

In 1995, President Bill Clinton signed Executive Order 12957 banning U.S. development of petroleum resources in Iran. Under congressional pressure, Clinton expanded U.S. financial measures against Iran by signing the Iran–Libya Sanctions Act of 1996 (ILSA, later renamed the Iran Sanctions Act), which authorized sanctions on foreign companies and individuals investing $20 million or more in one year in Iran's energy sector or selling threshold amounts of refined petroleum to Iran. In response to strong European objections, Clinton never invoked the sanctions.[28]

President George W. Bush expanded pressure against Iran by sanctioning Iranian banks. Financial measures were also imposed on the Revolutionary Guards and three of Iran's largest banks. The U.S. actions pressured other countries to sever financial transactions with these groups. Under President Obama, the U.S. has targeted Iran's energy sector— its principal source of exports—to degrade the government's finances and its nuclear weapons program. U.N. Security Council Resolution 1929 noted a "potential connection between Iran's revenues derived from its energy sector and the funding of Iran's proliferation-sensitive nuclear activities."[29]

Since 2010, the U.S., the EU, and U.N. have adopted steadily stricter and more comprehensive measures against Iran. In July 2010, Obama signed the Comprehensive

---

[26] Panel of Experts, "Report of the Panel of Experts Established Pursuant to Resolution 1874 (2009)," in U.N. Security Council, S/2013/337, June 11, 2013, p. 5, http://www.un.org/ga/search/view_doc.asp?symbol=S/2013/337.

[27] Ronald Reagan, "Prohibiting Imports from Iran," Executive Order 12613, October 29, 1987, http://www.archives.gov/federal-register/codification/executive-order/12613.html (accessed September 25, 2013).

[28] Bijan Khajehpour, Reza Marashi, and Trita Parsi, "Never Give In and Never Give Up," March 2013, http://www.niacouncil.org/site/DocServer/Never_give_in__never_give_up.pdf?docID=1941.

[29] U.N. Security Council, Resolution 1929 (2010), S/RES/1929 (2010), June 9, 2010, http://www.un.org/ga/search/view_doc.asp?symbol=S/RES/1929(2010).

Iran Sanctions, Accountability, and Divestment Act (CISADA), which prohibited providing fuel to Iran and banned the sale of equipment or services that would help Iran to increase its gasoline production capability.[30]

The National Defense Authorization Act of 2011 (NDAA) restricts foreign financial institutions' access to the U.S. financial system if they process petroleum transactions with Iran's central bank. The Iran Threat Reduction and Syria Human Rights Act of 2012 (ITRA) prohibits access to the U.S. market by companies doing business with Iran's energy sector and froze the U.S. assets of any entity doing business with the National Iranian Oil Company and the National Iranian Tanker Company.[31]

In June 2011, the Obama Administration sanctioned the Iranian security services for human rights abuses and the Islamic Republic of Iran Shipping Lines for proliferation activities. In November 2011, the Obama Administration issued Executive Order 13590 to expand U.S. financial measures on foreign companies that provided goods or services to Iran's oil and gas sector and petrochemical industry. Robert Einhorn, Obama's Special Advisor for Nonproliferation and Arms Control, cited Iran's progress toward enriching uranium, sponsorship of a plot to assassinate the Saudi ambassador in Washington, and human rights violations as reasons for imposing the tougher measures.[32]

In January 2013, the U.S. implemented new sanctions against Iran targeting key Iranian industries, such as shipping and ports management. The law also imposes sanctions on foreign companies that engage with Iranian companies in the targeted sectors.

The U.S. actions, combined with diplomatic pressure, led other nations to impose their own financial and regulatory measures against Iran, including an EU ban in 2012 against purchasing Iranian oil. Collectively, the international sanctions have isolated Iran from the international banking system, targeted critical Iranian economic sectors, and forced countries to restrict purchases of Iranian oil and gas, Tehran's largest export.

North Korea. The United Nations has imposed a series of incrementally tougher Security Council resolutions[33] on North Korea in response to Pyongyang's repeated defiance of previous resolutions. However, the U.N. did not pass any resolutions after Pyongyang's two attacks on South Korea in 2010.

The latest iteration, Resolution 2094:

---

[30] The Comprehensive Iran Sanctions, Accountability, and Divestment Act of 2010, Public Law 111–195, http://www.treasury.gov/resource-center/sanctions/Documents/hr2194.pdf.

[31] Khajehpour et al., "Never Give In and Never Give Up."

[32] Robert J. Einhorn, "U.S.–South Korea Relations," remarks at the American Center Korea, Seoul, December 5, 2011, http://iipdigital.usembassy.gov/st/english/texttrans/2011/12/20111207140416su0.157539.html.

[33] The U.N. Security Council passed Resolution 1695 in response to a North Korean missile test in 2006, Resolution 1718 in response to a North Korean nuclear test in 2006, Resolution 1874 in response to a North Korean nuclear test in 2009, Resolution 2087 in response to a North Korean missile test in 2012, and Resolution 2094 in response to a North Korean nuclear test in 2013.

- Demands that North Korea return at an early date to the Non-Proliferation Treaty;
- Reaffirms the U.N. demand that North Korea abandon all nuclear weapons, existing nuclear programs, and ballistic missile programs in a complete, verifiable, and irreversible manner;
- Decides that nations shall prevent any financial services, including electronic transfers through banks or their overseas correspondent accounts, that could contribute to North Korean nuclear or ballistic missile programs;
- Calls upon nations to prohibit North Korean financial institutions from establishing correspondent banks in their jurisdiction if reasonable grounds exist for believing that it could contribute to North Korean nuclear or missile programs; and
- Decides that nations shall inspect all cargo transiting their territory and deny permission to any aircraft flights if there are reasonable grounds for believing that it is related to prohibited North Korean programs.[34]

The United States has also issued a series of executive orders imposing punitive measures on North Korea.[35] In August 2010, the Obama Administration issued Executive Order 13551 to target North Korean arms trafficking and those engaged in illicit activities, including counterfeiting, narcotics smuggling, and money laundering. Executive Order 13570, issued in 2011, prohibits imports of North Korean goods into the United States unless licensed by the Office of Foreign Assets Control.

In 2010, Einhorn declared that North Korea was involved in "counterfeiting of U.S. currency and other goods, narcotics smuggling, and other illicit and deceptive activities in the international financial and banking systems [bringing] hundreds of millions of dollars in hard currency annually into North Korea, which can be used to support DPRK nuclear or missile programs."[36]

Pyongyang has repeatedly challenged Security Council resolutions with nuclear tests and ballistic missile launches. The continued existence of these programs is itself a violation of the resolutions. Pyongyang has made clear that it has no intention of complying with

---

[34] U.N. Security Council, Resolution 2094 (2013).

[35] George W. Bush, "Blocking Property and Prohibiting Transactions with Persons Who Commit, Threaten to Commit, or Support Terrorism," Executive Order 13224, September 23, 2001, http://georgewbush-whitehouse.archives.gov/news/releases/2001/09/20010924-1.html; George W. Bush, "Blocking Property of Weapons of Mass Destruction Proliferators and Their Supporters," Executive Order 13382, June 29, 2005, http://georgewbush-whitehouse.archives.gov/news/releases/2005/06/20050629.html; George W. Bush, "Continuing Certain Restrictions with Respect to North Korea and North Korean Nationals," Executive Order 13466, June 26, 2008, http://georgewbush-whitehouse.archives.gov/news/releases/2008/06/20080626-4.html; Barack Obama, "Blocking Property of Certain Persons with Respect to North Korea," Executive Order 13551, August 30, 2010, http://www.whitehouse.gov/the-press-office/2010/08/30/executive-order-president-blocking-property-certain-persons-with-respect; and Barack Obama, "Prohibiting Certain Transactions with Respect to North Korea," Executive Order 13570, April 18, 2011, http://www.whitehouse.gov/the-press-office/2011/04/18/executive-order-13570-prohibiting-certain-transactions-respect-north-kor.

[36] Robert J. Einhorn, "Terrorist Financing and Financial Crimes," remarks, U.S. Embassy, Seoul, August 2, 2010. http://www.state.gov/p/eap/rls/rm/2010/08/145598.htm (accessed September 26, 2013).

the U.N. resolutions or fulfilling its six-party-talks pledges to abandon its nuclear weapons. North Korea has declared that:

- "Pyongyang will not unilaterally abandon its war deterrence. North Korea's nuclear weapons are the ultimate defender of national interest and a trusted shield to defend peace."[37]
- Its nuclear weapons "are not goods for getting U.S. dollars and they are neither a political bargaining chip nor a thing for economic dealings. The DPRK's possession of nuclear weapons shall be fixed by law and the nuclear armed forces should be expanded and beefed up qualitatively and quantitatively."[38]
- "The six-party talks and the joint September 19 [2005] statement were rendered null and the denuclearization of the Korean Peninsula was put to an end. There will be no more discussion over denuclearization of the Korean Peninsula."[39]
- It is a "nuclear-armed state and an indomitable military power" in a revision of its constitution.[40]
- "Those who talk about an economic reward in return for the dismantlement of [North Korea's] nuclear weapons would be well advised to awake from their daydream."[41]
- "We have tightened our belts, braved various difficulties and spent countless amounts of money to obtain a nuclear deterrent as a self-defense measure against U.S. nuclear threats. Only fools will entertain the delusion that we will trade our nuclear deterrent for petty economic aid."[42]

China Critical to Sanction Success

The Iranian economy depends on global imports and exports, necessitating extensive international cooperation for sanctions to have an impact. Cooperation is complicated by Iran's status as a significant producer of oil, a critical world commodity that nations are loath to restrict.

Unlike Iran, North Korea is small, weak, and undiversified in its economic or diplomatic contacts. It is singularly reliant on China, making Pyongyang more susceptible to sanctions if Beijing or Chinese banks comply.

---

[37] Yonhap News Agency, "N. Korea Says No Plans to Give Up Nuclear Capabilities," May 28, 2013, http://english.yonhapnews.co.kr/northkorea/2013/05/28/92/0401000000AEN20130528008400315F.HTML

[38] Korean Central News Agency, "Report on Plenary Meeting of WPK Central Committee," Korea News Service (Tokyo), March 31, 2013, http://www.kcna.co.jp/item/2013/201303/news31/20130331-24ee.html.
[39] Yonhap News Agency, "Korea Vows to End Denuclearization Talks," January 23, 2013, http://english.yonhapnews.co.kr/northkorea/2013/01/23/95/0401000000AEN20130123001500315F.HTML

[40] Yonhap News Agency, "N.K. Calls Itself 'Nuclear-Armed State' in Revised Constitution," May 30, 2012, http://english.yonhapnews.co.kr/northkorea/2012/05/30/76/0401000000AEN20120530005200315F.HTML

[41] CNN, "North Korea Refuses to Abandon Nukes," February 19, 2010, http://www.cnn.com/2010/WORLD/asiapcf/02/19/north.korea.nuclear/index.html.
[42] Korea Herald/Asia News Network, "North Korea Pledges Not to Abandon Nukes," AsiaOne, February 21, 2010, http://news.asiaone.com/News/Latest+News/Asia/Story/A1Story20100221-199951.html.

North Korea's increased reliance on foreign-owned and foreign-flagged ships in recent years[43] provides an opportunity to improve interdiction of North Korean shipments. Foreign businesses and governments are more likely to allow inspection of their ships when confronted with evidence of North Korean malfeasance.

A Paper Dragon on Sanctions. Strong sanctions can work against a weak opponent, but coercive financial pressure against North Korea has been insufficiently robust and has been undermined by China. Despite North Korea's belligerent actions, Beijing is reluctant both to allow more comprehensive sanctions and to fully implement those already imposed:

- In 2002, Director of Central Intelligence George Tenet said that the proliferation activities of Chinese firms were at times "condoned by the Chinese government." In November 2007, the State Department assessed that shipments of prohibited North Korean missile parts "frequently transit Beijing on regularly scheduled flights" and that China failed to act on detailed information and a direct, personal appeal by President Bush.[44]
- After the April 2012 missile launch, the U.S., South Korea, Japan, and the EU proposed adding 40 additional North Korean entities to the U.N. sanctions list. China vetoed all but three, severely limiting the scope of U.N. efforts against North Korea's prohibited nuclear and missile programs. Despite the Chinese obstructionism, the Obama Administration hailed the addition of only three violators as a "strong and united response [that would] increase North Korea's isolation."[45]
- In 2013, U.S. and South Korean authorities found dozens of overseas bank accounts worth hundreds of millions of dollars that were linked to North Korean leaders Kim Jong-un and Kim Jong-il. Allied officials urged China to include these accounts in U.N. sanctions lists, but Beijing refused.[46] It is unclear why Washington and Seoul did not publicly identify the accounts and include them in their own unilateral sanctions.
- China has repeatedly increased its economic engagement with North Korea after the imposition of sanctions, thus negating their impact. After U.N. sanctions were first implemented in 2006, Chinese exports to North Korea actually increased by 140 percent by 2009.[47] In response to North Korea's sinking of the *Cheonan*, South Korea cut off most inter-Korean trade, worth approximately $300 million

---

[43] Mary Beth Nikitin et al., "Implementation of U.N. Security Council Resolution 1874," memorandum to Senator Richard G. Lugar (R–IN), October 8, 2010,
http://fpc.state.gov/documents/organization/152630.pdf.

[44] "Pyongyang's Accomplice," The Wall Street Journal, December 7, 2010,
http://online.wsj.com/article/SB10001424052748704594804575648473842565004.html.

[45] Voice of America News, "UN Expands Sanctions on N. Korea for Rocket Launch," Chosun Ilbo, May 3, 2012, http://english.chosun.com/site/data/html_dir/2012/04/17/2012041700398.html.

[46] "Kim Jong-un's Slush Funds Found," Chosun Ilbo, March 11, 2013,
http://english.chosun.com/site/data/html_dir/2013/03/11/2013031101105.html.

[47] Stephan Haggard and Marcus Noland, Famine in North Korea: Markets, Aid and Reform (New York: Columbia University Press, 2007), p. 230.

annually. Yet in the following year, China increased its trade with Pyongyang by 29 percent, from $2.68 billion to $3.47 billion.[48]

More robust Chinese implementation of sanctions will not guarantee that North Korea abandons its nuclear arsenal, but a continuation of Beijing's lackluster enforcement does guarantee that sanctions will fail to achieve their objectives.

Strong Sanctions, Effective When Applied

In 2005, U.S. criminal investigations Royal Charm and Smoking Dragon proved that North Korea was involved in drug smuggling and money laundering. The investigations also provided "incontrovertible proof of the role of Macao banks, Macao gangsters, and North Koreans in Macao," according to a senior State Department official.[49]

As a result, Washington declared Macao-based Banco Delta Asia (BDA) a primary money-laundering concern[50] and banned all U.S. financial institutions from dealing with BDA. The U.S. Department of the Treasury also considered implementing similar measures against other, larger banks, including the Macao branch of the Bank of China, against which it had "voluminous" evidence. However, the Bush Administration reportedly refrained to "avoid excessive damage to the financial system of Macao and a resultant clash with China."[51]

The U.S. action against BDA signaled that Washington would finally begin to enforce its laws. Taken in conjunction with *sub rosa* meetings by U.S. officials with Asian banks and businesses, it had a devastating impact on North Korea's finances. Foreign businesses and financial institutions shunned Pyongyang, fearful of being sanctioned as complicit in North Korean illegal activity. Two dozen financial institutions voluntarily cut back or terminated their business with North Korea, including institutions in China, Japan, Vietnam, Mongolia, and Singapore.[52]

The BDA targeted financial measures showed the efficacy of economic pressure tactics on North Korea. A North Korean deputy negotiator at the time quietly admitted to a senior White House official, "You finally found a way to hurt us."[53]

The United States eventually acquiesced to North Korea's demands that its ill-gotten money be returned. The Bush Administration even used the Federal Reserve Bank of

---

[48] Editorial, "Is China Neutralizing N. Korea Sanctions?" Chosun Ilbo, May 23, 2011, http://english.chosun.com/site/data/html_dir/2011/05/23/2011052301184.html

[49] Donald Greenlees and David Lague, "The Money Trail That Linked North Korea to Macao," The New York Times, April 11, 2007, http://www.nytimes.com/2007/04/11/world/asia/11cnd-macao.html.

[50] Under the Patriot Act, § 311, 31 U.S. Code § 5318A.

[51] Greenlees and Lague, "The Money Trail That Linked North Korea to Macao."

[52] Daniel L. Glaser, testimony before the Committee on Banking, Housing, and Urban Affairs, U.S. Senate, September 12, 2006, http://www.banking.senate.gov/public/index.cfm?FuseAction=Files.View&FileStore_id=deda4b45-d225-4a22-8ec4-2154cbc61ded.

[53] Juan Zarate, *Treasury's War: The Unleashing of a New Era of Financial Warfare*, Public Affairs, New York, 2013.

New York to transfer the money since no U.S. commercial bank dared to risk involvement in felony money laundering.

At the time, critics derided the BDA law enforcement initiative as a neoconservative attempt to undermine the six-party nuclear negotiations. Yet senior Obama Administration officials privately characterized the initiative as having been "very effective" and argued that President George Bush's decision to rescind it was "a mistake that eased pressure on Pyongyang before it took irreversible steps to dismantle its nuclear program."[54] The Obama Administration now "hopes to recreate the financial pressure that North Korea endured back in 2005 when [the United States] took the action against Banco Delta Asia."[55]

Costs of Timidity

Regrettably, the world has now become largely inured to North Korea's development of nuclear weapons, repeated violations of Security Council resolutions and international law, and belligerent threats. Evidence of North Korean nuclear and missile progress has often been dismissed until it became irrefutable.

After each North Korean provocation or violation, the U.S. and its allies returned to the Security Council demanding stronger measures, only to run into Chinese obfuscation and obstruction. The result has been only incrementally strengthened measures.

Instead, the U.N. and U.S. should have imposed comprehensive sanctions against North Korea and its facilitators immediately after Pyongyang's provocations, when international outrage and support was strongest. The Obama Administration's policy of strategic patience is predominantly passive because it fails to impose sufficient pressure to effectively degrade North Korea's capabilities or alter its behavior. The U.S. has sufficient tools. It has just lacked the resolve to use them.

In 2010, President Obama declared that the United States will "continue to press on sanctions implementation until there is concrete, verifiable progress on denuclearization," but Administration officials privately commented that year that the "intensity with which they push for tough implementation of sanctions [is] calibrated depending" on North Korean behavior.[56] In March 2013, despite North Korea's repeated violations of U.N. resolutions, a State Department official commented that there was still room to increase sanctions on North Korea: "[W]e haven't maxed out, there is headroom."[57]

The obvious question is: Why has the Obama Administration not lowered the boom on Pyongyang as it has on Iran, instead preferring to keep some financial pressure measures

---

[54] Jay Solomon, "U.S. Pursues Financial Leverage over North Korea," The Wall Street Journal, July 1, 2009, http://online.wsj.com/article/SB124632106686771095.html.

[55] Margaret Brenan, "U.S. Urges Nations to Cut North Korea's Financial Link," CBS News, April 5, 2013, http://webcache.googleusercontent.com/search?q=cache:n3xFhCvg6QAJ:www.cbsnews.com/8301-202_162-57578210/u.s-urges-nations-to-cut-north-koreas-financial-link.

[56] Nikitin et al., "Implementation of U.N. Security Council Resolution 1874."

[57] Adrian Croft, "U.S. Wants EU to Put North Korean Bank on Sanctions List," Reuters, March 25, 2013, http://www.reuters.com/article/2013/03/25/us-korea-north-cu-idUSBRE92O0TU20130325.

in reserve for another incremental step after the next North Korean provocation? For example, sanctioning North Korea's Foreign Trade Bank in 2013 is an effective measure, but why was it not done several years earlier?

Sanctions have delayed North Korea's nuclear and missile programs. Punitive measures have caused international financial institutions and businesses to become increasingly reluctant to engage with North Korea, even in legitimate businesses. Coercive financial pressure has raised the risk and cost to Pyongyang and its facilitators and forced them to alter their operations, thus stretching out the development timelines.

However, by adopting a sanctions policy of timid incrementalism, the U.S. squandered the opportunity to impede progress on North Korea's nuclear and missile programs more effectively and coerce compliance with U.N. resolutions. The regime has successfully weathered weak diplomatic responses to its provocations, weak international sanctions, and no military response to its two attacks on South Korea. As a result, Pyongyang feels that its own strategic patience policy can outlast that of its opponents.

The collective international finger-wagging and promises to be tougher the next time have allowed North Korea additional years to develop and refine its nuclear weapons and the means to deliver them. The inability and unwillingness to impose more comprehensive sanctions has emboldened North Korea, Iran, and other nuclear aspirants to believe they can defy the world until they present their nuclear status as a fait accompli. North Korea also has felt no compunction about proliferating nuclear and chemical weapon technologies to Syria.

What Should Be Done
The United States should increase punitive measures against North Korea, including enhancing sanctions to the same degree as they have been applied against other rogue regimes, such as Iran today and Burma at key points.

The United States should unilaterally:

- **Designate North Korea as a primary money-laundering concern.** In 2002, 2004, and 2011, the U.S. Treasury designated Ukraine, Burma, and Iran, respectively, as "jurisdiction[s] of primary money laundering concern" under Section 311 of the USA Patriot Act.[58]
- **Ban North Korean financial institutions' correspondent accounts[59] in the United States.** Designating North Korea (like Burma and Iran) as a money-

---

[58] U.S. Department of the Treasury, "Imposition of Special Measures Against Burma," April 2, 2004, in Federal Register, Vol. 69, No. 70 (April 12, 2004), pp. 19093–19098, http://www.fincen.gov/statutes_regs/patriot/pdf/burma.pdf (accessed September 26, 2013), and press release, "Fact Sheet: New Sanctions on Iran," U.S. Department of the Treasury, November 21, 2011, http://www.treasury.gov/press-center/press-releases/Pages/tg1367.aspx.
[59] "Foreign financial institutions maintain accounts at U.S. banks to gain access to the U.S. financial system and to take advantage of services and products that may not be available in the foreign financial institution's jurisdiction." Federal Financial Institutions Examination Council, Bank Secrecy Act/Anti-

laundering concern under Section 311 of the Patriot Act would prohibit North Korea from "the opening or maintaining in the United States of a correspondent account or payable-through account by any domestic financial institution or domestic financial agency for or on behalf of a foreign banking institution."[60] Executive Order 13310 prohibited "the exportation or reexportation, directly or indirectly, to Burma of any financial services either from the United States or by a United States person."[61] Even financial institutions not doing business in the United States would likely be affected since "nearly all dollar-denominated transactions pass through U.S. Treasury-regulated banks. Chinese and European banks that need their own access to U.S. financial institutions may also shun transactions with North Korea."[62]

- **Publicly identify and sanction all foreign companies, financial institutions, and governments assisting North Korea's nuclear and missile programs.** Executive Orders 13382 and 13551 enable targeted financial and regulatory measures, including freezing of assets, against any entity suspected of helping North Korean nuclear, missile, and conventional arms; criminal activities; money laundering; or import of luxury goods.[63] The U.S. should call on foreign banks, businesses, and governments to reciprocate U.S. actions against North Korean and foreign violators.

- **Impose third-party sanctions.** The U.S. should penalize entities, particularly Chinese financial institutions and businesses, that trade with those on the sanctions list or export prohibited items. The U.S. should also ban financial institutions that conduct business with North Korea from conducting business in the United States.[64]

- **Compel the removal of North Korea from SWIFT financial transfers.** The Obama Administration and European Union pressured the Belgian-based Society for Worldwide Interbank Financial Telecommunication (SWIFT) to disconnect sanctioned Iranian banks in 2012. The system is the world hub for electronic financial transactions.

Money Laundering InfoBase, s.v. "Correspondent Accounts (Foreign)—Overview." http://www.ffiec.gov/bsa_aml_infobase/pages_manual/OLM_047.htm.

[60] U.S. Department of the Treasury, Financial Crimes Enforcement Network, "Section 311—Special Measures," http://www.fincen.gov/statutes_regs/patriot/section311.html.

[61] George W. Bush, "Blocking Property of the Government of Burma and Prohibiting Certain Transactions." Executive Order 13310, July 28, 2003, http://www.gpo.gov/fdsys/pkg/FR-2003-07-30/pdf/03-19573.pdf.

[62] Joshua Stanton, "Kaesong Investors Beware: Treasury Issues New Warning About N. Korea Money Laundering Risk," September 21, 2013, http://freekorea.us/2013/09/21/kaesong-investors-beware-treasury-issues-new-warning-about-n-korea-money-laundering-risk/.

[63] Sung-Yoon Lee and Joshua Stanton, "Hit Kim Jong Eun Where It Hurts: His Wallet," The Washington Post, February 13, 2013, http://articles.washingtonpost.com/2013-02-12/opinions/37059212_1_nuclear-test-pyongyang-international-network.

[64] Executive Order 13551 applies U.S. sanctions to anyone that has assisted "any person whose property and interests in property are blocked pursuant to this order." Barack Obama, "Blocking Property of Certain Persons with Respect to North Korea," Executive Order 13551, § 1(a)(ii) (E), http://www.whitehouse.gov/the-press-office/2010/08/30/executive-order-president-blocking-property-certain-persons-with-respect.

- **Urge the European Union and other countries to sever ties with North Korea's Foreign Trade Bank.** The Foreign Trade Bank, North Korea's main financial portal for international trade, was blacklisted by the U.S. and China in 2013 for facilitating North Korean nuclear and missile proliferation.
- **Target the North Korean government writ large, not just individuals or departments.** The U.S. determined in Executive Order 13551 that the North Korean government itself was involved in illicit and deceptive activities.[65]
- **Formally charge North Korea as a currency counterfeiter.** U.S. officials have repeatedly declared that North Korea is counterfeiting U.S. currency.[66] Under international law, counterfeiting of a country's currency "qualifies as a proxy attack on its national integrity and sovereignty – and a *causus belli* to justify self-defense."[67]
- **Resume law enforcement efforts against North Korean illicit activities.** Despite the U.S. government's affirmation that North Korea is complicit in the counterfeiting of currency and pharmaceuticals, illegal production and distribution of narcotics, and money laundering, the U.S. apparently has not taken any law enforcement action since the mid-2000s when the Banco Delta Asia money was returned. Pyongyang's involvement in illicit activities should trigger criminal cases against the North Korean leadership.
- **Return North Korea to the state sponsors of terrorism list.** North Korea has provided missile and nuclear assistance to Iran and Syria, two nations on the U.S. State Department's Sponsors of Terrorism List.[68] North Korean weapons seized in Thailand were headed for Islamist groups Hamas and Hezbollah. Two North Korean agents confessed that Kim Young-chol, chief of the Reconnaissance Bureau, ordered them to assassinate Hwang Jang-yop, the highest-ranking North Korean defector.[69] Inclusion on the list requires the U.S. government to oppose loans by international financial institutions, such as the World Bank, International Monetary Fund, and Asian Development Bank.[70]
- **Tighten maritime counterproliferation.** The U.S. should target shipping companies and airlines caught proliferating. If they are state-owned, the U.S.

---

[65] Executive Order 13551 concludes by "finding that the continued actions and policies of the Government of North Korea, |including| its illicit and deceptive activities in international markets through which it obtains financial and other support, including money laundering, the counterfeiting of goods and currency, bulk cash smuggling, and narcotics trafficking ... constitute an unusual and extraordinary threat to the national security, foreign policy, and economy of the United States." Ibid. (emphasis added).

[66] Phillip Crowley, daily press briefing, U.S. Department of State, August 2, 2010, http://www.state.gov/r/pa/prs/dpb/2010/08/145491.htm.

[67] Zarate, *Treasury's War.*

[68] Countries that the Secretary of State determines have repeatedly provided support for acts of international terrorism are designated pursuant to three laws: Section 6(j) of the Export Administration Act, Section 40 of the Arms Export Control Act, and Section 620A of the Foreign Assistance Act. U.S. Department of State, "State Sponsors of Terrorism." http://www.state.gov/j/ct/list/c14151.htm.

[69] Kim So-hyun, "Kim Visits Army Unit Spying on S. Korea," The Korea Herald, April 27, 2010, http://www.koreaherald.com/national/Detail.jsp?newsMLId=20100427000663.

[70] Section 1621, "Opposition to Assistance by International Financial Institutions to Terrorist States," of the International Financial Institutions Act (Public Law 95–118), as cited in Mark E. Manyin, "North Korea: Back on the Terrorism List?" Congressional Research Service Report for Congress, June 29, 2010, http://www.nkeconwatch.com/nk-uploads/DPRK-back-on-terrorism-list.pdf.

should sanction the relevant government ministry. Sanctions have been applied against the Islamic Republic of Iran Shipping Line and Iran Air.

- **Enhance U.S. inspection of shipping companies transiting ports that consistently fail to inspect North Korean cargo.** Any vessel or aircraft that has transported prohibited North Korea items should be seized upon entering U.S. jurisdiction.

In the U.N., the U.S. should press the Security Council to:

- **Close loopholes in Resolution 2094,** such as including Article 42 of Chapter VII of the U.N. Charter, which allows for enforcement by military means. This would authorize naval ships to intercept, board, and inspect North Korean ships suspected of transporting precluded nuclear, missile, and conventional arms, components, or technology.
- **Adopt a more comprehensive list of prohibited items and materials.** The U.N. Experts Group identified several items and materials critical to Pyongyang's nuclear programs that should be—but have not been—added to the list of products banned for transfer to North Korea. These include maraging steel, frequency changers (also known as converters or inverters), high-strength aluminum alloy, filament winding machines, ring magnets, and semi-hard magnetic alloys in thin strip form.[71]
- **Constrain trade of major North Korean imports and exports.** The U.S. should apply sanctions similar to those imposed on significant Iran imports and exports. The U.S. should also restrict North Korean energy imports and the export of North Korean resources. U.S. law restricts access to the U.S. financial system by foreign companies and banks if they do business with Iran's energy sector or process petroleum transactions with Iran's central bank.

Time for Incrementalism Is Past
North Korea is every bit the nuclear threat that Iran is. In fact, in terms of real capabilities, it is an even greater threat today to its neighbors than Iran is to its neighbors. North Korea's successful missile and nuclear tests show that in only a matter of time, Pyongyang will be able to threaten the United States directly with nuclear weapons.

North Korea already threatens U.S. interests and allies in Asia. The regime shows its disdain for international efforts to constrain its behavior by openly and repeatedly defying international law and U.N. resolutions. Responding with strong rhetoric and minimalist measures has only encouraged North Korea to remain on course.

North Korea faces a perfect storm of conditions that makes it more vulnerable to economic pressure. The U.S. and its allies are unwilling to offer unconditional benefits without progress in the six-party talks. International aid has been curtailed due to Pyongyang's refusal to accept global monitoring standards, and international coercive financial pressure is affecting North Korea's finances. This increasing economic isolation could lead the regime to become more malleable.

---

[71] Panel of Experts, "Report of the Panel of Experts Established Pursuant to Resolution 1874 (2009)."

The United States possesses an array of strong punitive measures that it can levy on Pyongyang. It has employed many of these against Iran. The Obama Administration should overcome its reluctance to impose more extensive punitive measures against Pyongyang and the foreign entities that assist its nuclear and missile programs. It should also make clear to the new Chinese leadership that continued sheltering of its recalcitrant ally will only increase the potential for a crisis on the Korean Peninsula.

Washington should no longer hold some sanctions in abeyance, to be rolled out after the next North Korean violation or provocation. There will be little change until North Korea feels pain and China feels concern over the consequences of Pyongyang's actions and its own obstructionism.

****

The Heritage Foundation is the most broadly supported think tank in the United States. During 2013, it had more than 600,000 individual, foundation, and corporate supporters representing every state in the U.S. Its 2013 operating income came from the following sources:

Individuals	80%
Foundations	17%
Corporations	3%

The top five corporate givers provided The Heritage Foundation with 1% of its 2013 operating income. The Heritage Foundation's books are audited annually by the national accounting firm of McGladrey & Pullen. A list of major donors is available from The Heritage Foundation upon request.

Mr. CHABOT. Thank you very much. We appreciate the testimony from all three of the witnesses here this afternoon. I'd now like to recognize the gentleman from the Commonwealth of Virginia, Mr. Connolly, for the purpose of making an opening statement.

Mr. CONNOLLY. Thank you so much, Mr. Chairman. I appreciate very much your holding this hearing. I also appreciate the testimony particularly of Ms. Grace Jo, and just listening to what she went through and her family went through. Thank you so much for the courage of testifying today.

I'm also, Mr. Chairman, delighted that the chairman of the committee has announced that we're going to actually markup H.R. 1771, North Korean Sanctions. And, Mr. Klingner, am I pronouncing that right? Thank you for your list, very helpful, because I think they do need to have teeth.

Two points I would just make, Mr. Chairman, listening to this panel. One is, it is imperative that the United States put teeth into the sanctions it imposes in the North. They should never be less than what they are with some other rogue states. And, secondly, we may have an opportunity with respect to China, and I know we're going to explore that on this panel. But the fact of the matter is, when Kim Jong-un executed his uncle, he executed the Chief Interlocutor with the People's Republic of China. And in doing that, perhaps the Chinese got the message that their longstanding policy with respect to North Korea may no longer be tenable. And that may give us a diplomatic opportunity. And, again, I very much look forward to talking with the panel about that.

Mr. Chairman, thank you so much for the opportunity.

Mr. CHABOT. Thank you very much. I'll now begin by recognizing myself for 5 minutes for the purpose of asking questions.

China's policy toward North Korea, and Mr. Connolly already alluded to this, appears to have undergone some evolution in the year since Xi took office. In some instances, appearing to be more willing to express its displeasure with Pyongyang. What, if anything, can be done to influence China, who is, after all, the key here and has the most influence to pressure North Korea, to lean on them to civilize itself. That seems to be beyond the capability of this regime but to at least be less oppressive to its people than it currently is? I would welcome any of the witnesses to talk to us about that. Mr. Klingner.

Mr. KLINGNER. Yes, sir. As I said, there were hopes that Xi Jinping would be different, and a year ago during the time when North Korea was heightening tensions to a dangerous level it appeared China was more angry with its recalcitrant ally. Since then, since North Korea has shifted back to a charm offensive, we've seen Beijing sort of walk back from those initial positive hopeful steps.

Most recently, we've seen China has rejected the U.N. Commission of Inquiry's Human Rights Report saying its "divorced from reality," and they have refused U.N. action to refer it either to the ICC or a tribunal. We have seen in the past, China has turned a blind eye to proliferation that transited its country—North Korean missile parts, for example, going to Iran. We've seen it refuse to take actions when the U.S. Government even provided information.

It did recently take action, it severed financial relations with North Korea's Financial Trade Bank. It had done this a decade ago, and then undid that action, so there are a number of things China has done, but then undid them. So, again, I think we need a focus on a unilateral U.S. strategy rather than on China in the U.N. Security Council.

Mr. CHABOT. Thank you. Mr. Scarlatoiu, did you want to add anything to that?

Mr. SCARLATOIU. Certainly, Mr. Chairman. China is an aspiring super power that helped establish and maintain the Kim regime in power for more than 60 years. In a letter addressed to the President of China, the Commission of Inquiry made it clear that by its policy of forcibly returning North Korean refugees to conditions of danger, China puts itself in a position where it is aiding and abetting a regime that has committed crimes against humanity.

Certainly, as Mr. Klingner has pointed out, the recommendation that the Security Council submit, refer the case to the International Criminal Court is unlikely to happen over the short to medium term, in particular because of a potential Chinese veto.

For what it's worth, we might as well push the Chinese and place them in a position where they actually have to exercise their right to veto as a permanent member of the Security Council, further reinforcing the clear impression that China is aiding and abetting a regime that has committed crimes against humanity.

Mr. CHABOT. Thank you very much. Ms. Jo, if I could turn to you now, and ask you a different question. As a refugee yourself, could you share with us your insights about the obstacles that you faced obtaining refugee status in the U.S., and about the humanitarian conditions that North Korean refugees face, in general?

Ms. JO. Yes, sir. As a refugee our family has lived in the United States almost 6 years now. And in the beginning we had support from the government, about 8 months, which is Medicare and Food Stamps, and cash about $250 for each person, so that helps our family a lot. And I believe most of the refugees they do get same benefits as our family.

The one thing I would like to ask government to support refugee, which is North Korean refugees, is we need some sort of organization to support new refugees to educate them in society, and in America, the language different, and society is different. It's very difficult to assimilate in the society as a refugee, so I don't know is there any organization we can educate them, but I would like to ask government to support some organization to educate them and support them about a year or year and a half to help them to know the United States. Thank you.

Mr. CHABOT. Thank you very much. I appreciate it. My time has expired. The gentleman from California, Mr. Sherman, is recognized for 5 minutes.

Mr. SHERMAN. Ms. Jo, thank you for your courage and for telling us your story.

Mr. Klingner, how many nuclear weapons, and I realize this is unclassified and just does North Korea have, or at least have enough fissile material to create? And can you tell us the status of uranium and plutonium programs to create additional weapons?

Mr. KLINGNER. Well, sir, the information on North Korea is very difficult to get. Even when I was in the intelligence community, we referred to it as the hardest of the hard targets. But I think experts generally assess that North Korea likely has six to eight pluto-nium-based nuclear weapons. The uranium program I believe is much further along than some believe it has achieved because it has been underway since the late 1980s. It also received critical support from Pakistan and the A.Q. Khan Network. There's been a rogues gallery of interaction with Iran, Pakistan, A.Q. Khan, Libya, and North Korea where they exchanged valuable informa-tion and components. So, I think in return for North Korea assist-ance on putting warheads onto short and medium-range missile to Pakistan, Pakistan replied by providing centrifuges and critical——

Mr. SHERMAN. So, their plutonium program generated enough fissile material, from six to eight weapons, and the consensus seems to be that that program is not producing any more fissile material?

Mr. KLINGNER. It has been dormant for some years, but we've seen just in the last year from unclassified satellite imagery that North Korea is expanding its uranium reprocessing facilities. The reactor program at Yongbyon, as well as two very extensive missile launch facilities on the east and the west coast.

The latest missile test, I'm sorry, the latest nuclear test may have been uranium, but we were unable to determine whether it was plutonium.

Mr. SHERMAN. I would point out that there's a focus on missiles, even missile defense. And, obviously, the highest status for a dic-tator is to have a nuclear tipped intercontinental ballistic missile, but the less prestigious way to deliver a nuclear weapon is to smuggle one, and you can easily smuggle one into the United States inside a bale of marijuana.

We're not safe from this. We declared that it was unacceptable for North Korea to have a nuclear weapon, and then went to sleep pretty much. So, we are now in a position where it may be in our interest to negotiate with a terrible regime and to provide the kind of aid that Mr. Rohrabacher would decry if there was a way to limit them to their current six to eight plutonium-based weapons. The only thing worse than North Korea with six to eight weapons is a North Korea with 16 to 18 weapons.

Has the North Korean Government shown any interest in even limiting, let alone disgorging, the fruits of its nuclear weapons pro-gram, Mr. Klingner?

Mr. KLINGNER. No, sir. They made very clear under Kim Jong-il, and now under Kim Jong-un that they have no intention of abandoning their nuclear arsenal. They have repeatedly——

Mr. SHERMAN. Of abandoning or even failing to augment, or just they have no intention to abandon, or no intention to fail to aug-ment?

Mr. KLINGNER. Right. They have violated the four previous agreements that they signed to never pursue a nuclear weapons program. They violated the three agreements to denuclearize. They've indicated no indication that they want to pursue that.

Mr. SHERMAN. So, we have no reason not to follow every one of your suggestions as to how to impose additional sanctions.

Mr. KLINGNER. What I recommend is, as part of a comprehensive integrated strategy, using conditional engagement, and also more effective punitive measures to try to compel them to return to their denuclearization commitments. And then since perhaps those two——

Mr. SHERMAN. Well, the problem we have on denuclearization is Gaddafi gave up his nuclear program which was more advanced than we realized. Saddam gave up his weapons of mass destruction, the Ukraine gave up the third largest nuclear arsenal. Gaddafi and Saddam are dead, and Ukraine doesn't have Crimea. It's going to be very hard to convince any country that has nuclear weapons to give them up given that track record.

We may be able, though, to halt progress toward future weapons whether it be Iran, which is still at zero, or North Korea, but I think that goal of a non-nuclear North Korea is a goal we should have stuck to, and didn't. But I thank you for outlining the possible actions we could take to try to create a verifiable destruction of those tools that they are using, particularly in the uranium area, to expand their stockpile of nuclear weapons. And given how this regime treats its own people, it's pretty important to make sure they don't have even more. I yield back.

Mr. CHABOT. Thank you. The gentleman's time has expired. The gentleman from Pennsylvania, Mr. Perry, is recognized for 5 minutes.

Mr. PERRY. Thank you, Mr. Chairman.

Mr. Scarlatoiu, what would you characterize as the successes of our policy of Strategic Patience?

Mr. SCARLATOIU. Mr. Perry, certainly in our area of human rights, unfortunately the greatest challenge that we face is that we have paid a lot of attention to the very important political security challenges that we face on the Korean Peninsula, but not the human rights considerations.

I think that we need to take those concerns into account because concern for human rights is part of who we are, because these are values that we share with our friends, partners, and allies in Northeast Asia and beyond, in particular, with——

Mr. PERRY. Let me—pardon my interruption, but let me rephrase it.

So, are there any successes, strategic, tactical, nuclear, human rights, are there any successes to this strategy that you can enumerate for me?

Mr. SCARLATOIU. As far as I can see, there are no successes, Congressman Perry. As far as I can see, the policy of Strategic Patience is one of very few, if any, available options that we have under the current circumstances, in particular, because North Korea has entirely lost its international credibility, as Mr. Klingner was mentioning, by joining the non-proliferation treaty, pulling out of the non-proliferation treaty, joining the Geneva Agreed Framework, pulling out, most recently in 2012 agreeing to the leap day agreement, then two and a half——

Mr. PERRY. Right. I mean, we know that they don't honor any of their commitments. I'm just—I'm frustrated, I think as many Americans are, that what we're doing is just kind of sitting back and waiting to see what happens; meanwhile, the things that Ms.

Jo enumerated are occurring on a minutely, instantaneous basis every hour of the day. And it breaks our heart to know that, and know that we're literally doing nothing about it. Let me move on.

Mr. Klingner, how do you view the international interim nuclear deal with Iran in relation to the North Korean nuclear problem? Do you see any juxtaposition, does one have any effect on the other, or does one incentivize North Korea in a certain way, or not? Is there any interplay whatsoever in your mind?

Mr. KLINGNER. Well, in reviewing the interim agreement, I certainly had a case of deja vu having followed North Korea for 20 years. I think there are lessons that we've learned from negotiating with North Korea that should be applied with Iran. I think we need very extensive, very detailed negotiations or agreements like we had with the Soviet Union in the Warsaw Pact. We need very, very stringent verification measures to insure that North Korea or Iran is not cheating, as North Korea repeatedly has done in the past.

We need to have the willingness to walk away from the table if it's a bad deal. I think in the past with North Korea we often saw, as one negotiator put it, the desire to keep the bicycle moving. If it stops, it falls over, so the negotiations were kept going for the sake of——

Mr. PERRY. So, we learned, but in essence we—I mean, learning is this—I would think you would take a different action based on what you learned from the mistakes that you learned. But we have the information, we know what was successful, we know what failed, but we haven't applied any of that in Iran, if I could be succinct about your answer.

Mr. KLINGNER. I think the lessons are there. Whether we've learned them is a different story.

Mr. PERRY. All right. Do you accept the assessment of the U.S. Intelligence Committee that North Korea will be deterred from using nuclear weapons except possibly in the scenario of imminent regime collapse?

Mr. KLINGNER. I would largely agree. I think they realize that using nuclear weapons would bring about the end of their regime and the end of their country. I think their nuclear weapons are intended more for compellence or coercion. The U.S. and South Korea have been deterred from responding to military attacks that North Korea has committed in the past even before they had nuclear weapons. And now that they have nuclear weapons, North Korea would think that they could get away with more than they did before.

Mr. PERRY. Okay, thank you. I will tell you that I—as other members of the panel listened intently to your list of potential options for the United States, and I'll be working with the chairman and the other members of the committee to help draft that legislation, partly due to the list that you've provided, or with that in mind, because I think it would be very helpful.

Just in the time remaining, Ms. Jo, your story is incredibly compelling, and I could tell you, I think it breaks everyone's heart in the room, and if every American could hear it, it would break their heart. But from your point of view, and I understand you've been gone a long time, and you were there as child, but the things you've seen and endured, what from your perspective would make a difference to turn that leadership around, to turn—to have the people rise up against this oppression, to completely change the situation in North Korea? What will motivate—is there anything that could motivate the people? Is there any chance for the people to do this on their own, and some way for the United States and the United Nations to motivate that, empower that, encourage that?

Ms. Jo. Politically, I don't have full educated, so I cannot give you the exact answer. But in my opinion and thinking, the United States, we can help the Ministries or the individual people who already escaped into China, who are seeking freedom. So, we can rescue refugees in China to the freedom country. And once we rescue hundreds, thousands refugees from North Korea, I believe one day North Korean regime will fall down.

Mr. CHABOT. Thank you very much, and thank you for your answer.

Ms. Jo. Thank you.

Mr. CHABOT. We appreciate that. The gentleman from Virginia, Mr. Connolly, is recognized for 5 minutes.

Mr. CONNOLLY. Thank you, Mr. Chairman.

Mr. Klingner, first of all, I don't—it's not often I find myself in near total agreement with the Heritage Foundation, but I must say I found your testimony right on, and very helpful in terms of not just providing a critique of U.S. policy, but giving us a roadmap for how we might become much more efficacious. And I thank you for that contribution, as well, and I echo what my colleagues said.

I think when—I've written the chairman requesting a markup of H.R. 1771, and we're going to do that. And when we do, we certainly will take a very close, hard look at your recommendations, so this hearing is very timely.

Let me ask you about China. How important do you think China is to the ultimate issue of North Korea and ultimate reunification? Conventional wisdom had it that the Chinese would never support reunification, that having the hermit kingdom sort of under their thumb served their interest, keeping the peninsula divided served their interest, but you could make the case that perhaps in light of recent events and, frankly, the opening up of the Chinese economy, they have a lot more in common with the South than they do with the North. And that the North has now become an albatross more than anything else. And in this case even a sort of unpredictable albatross, if such a thing exists. I don't know if albatrosses can be unpredictable, Mr. Chairman, but let's assume they can. Especially in light of the execution of Kim Jong-un's uncle.

So, how important is China? What leverage do they have? And are we—do we have reason to believe as the United States that they might be more open to our importunings than in the past?

Mr. KLINGNER. You ask a very good question, sir, because experts on China and North Korea have been struggling with that, and we haven't come to an answer.

The Chinese-North Korean relationship is complicated, and what we've seen in China, even at the senior leadership level, is a split between, if you will, old school who support their ally and alliance forged in blood, and the younger leadership who sees, as you pointed out, North Korea is an albatross. The future of China on the Korean Peninsula is with the South for economic reasons, so there is that struggle. But to date, the old school has outvoted the new school.

As for unification, the Bush administration, the Obama administration, and Track II discussions outside of government have tried to get China to articulate what are its red lines, what are its thoughts toward unification, would it accept it? What would cause it to go into North Korea? And China has been resistant, so that lack of transparency is very concerning to U.S. and South Korean policy makers.

Just yesterday when Xi Jinping met with Park Eun Ji, he seemed to indicate acceptance of unification or support for President Park's unification approach. We don't know how much we can take that to the bank. One would hope China would acquiesce to a Korean unification, but we don't know. And that uncertainty is of great concern to the United States.

Mr. CONNOLLY. What is the remaining leverage Beijing has on Pyongyang?

Mr. KLINGNER. Although it has the most leverage of any country in the world on North Korea, its amount of leverage is less than perhaps people think. Of course, you can point to the overwhelming majority of economic engagement from North Korea to China, it's its largest trading partner. You know, people say China could cut off the food and the fuel, but China is unlikely to do that. That would create a crisis on the border, which is what they want to avoid.

So, I think what the U.S. needs to do is point out to China that its refusal or its resistance to putting pressure on North Korea is bringing about the very crisis it doesn't want. It's encouraging North Korea to pursue these nuclear programs and missile programs, to engage in deadly acts of attack on South Korea, which will bring about U.S. and South Korean military responses that Beijing doesn't want. We need to make clear to Beijing that it can act now, or it can act later.

Mr. CONNOLLY. One can also say that, I suppose, of the kind of situation Grace Jo described. I mean, returning North Korean refugees who get into China back to the North Korean regime is virtually a death sentence, and certainly a terrible blemish on the Chinese record. And one wonders whether the Chinese think that continuing that policy makes any sense in light of the brutality and the lack of international acceptance of the North and its behavior by any norms at all.

Mr. KLINGNER. Right. As my colleagues can address far better, is that forced repatriation is itself in violation of international accords.

Mr. CONNOLLY. If the chairman would allow Mr. Scarlatoiu to address the questions, then I will relent.

Mr. CHABOT. Sure. The gentleman's time is expired, but Mr. Scarlatoiu can respond.

Mr. CONNOLLY. I thank the chair.

Mr. SCARLATOIU. Thank you, Congressman Connolly.

China joined in 1982 the U.N. Refugee Convention, the 1951 Refugee Convention. Pursuant to that Convention, if a person is repatriated and faces conditions of danger, then that person automatically qualifies to be granted access to the process leading to acquiring political refugee status. We have had numerous credible reports of North Koreans who were forcibly returned by China, especially those who came in contact with South Koreans or Christian missionaries along the road of defection were tortured, beaten, imprisoned in political prison camps, North Korean women who became pregnant with Chinese men along the road of defection, were subjected to sexual violence, rape. We have credible reports of infanticide, forced abortions.

China continues this policy of forcible repatriation of North Koreans claiming that they're illegal economic migrants. Last week in Geneva on the 17th of March, right after the submission and the presentation of the report of the U.N. Commission of Inquiry by Judge Michael Kirby of Australia, China again stated that these North Korean refugees are not political refugees, but illegal economic migrants which makes absolutely no sense, and is a flagrant violation of the 1951 Refugee Convention.

Mr. CHABOT. Thank you. The gentleman's time has expired. We'll go into a second round in case any other members have questions. We're going to have votes here shortly, so just a couple of quick questions.

Mr. Scarlatoiu and Mr. Klingner, let me ask you this first question: You both mentioned the need for more effective and targeted sanctions against North Korea that link sanctions to North Korea's human rights abuses. And we've mentioned the legislation that's being contemplated here, H.R. 1771. Could you touch briefly on what in H.R. 1771 you like that may actually have some impact? Mr. Scarlatoiu?

Mr. SCARLATOIU. Chairman Chabot, the Committee for Human Rights in North Korea recognizes that the North Korea Sanctions Enforcement Act of 2013 addresses not only North Korea's nuclear and missile programs, but also identifies human rights violations as conduct that is subject to sanctions.

The Committee for Human Rights in North Korea appreciates that H.R. 1771 also insures that humanitarian assistance to North Korea is not affected by the sanctions in the spirit of targeted sanctions called for by the recently released report of the U.N. Commission of Inquiry.

We are aware that the revised draft of the legislation actually insures that funds that would otherwise have been used by the North Korean regime to purchase ski lifts, luxury goods, weapons and missile components will be used for the purchase of humanitarian supplies, food, and medicine for those who need it most for the North Korean people. It is certainly also important to insure that humanitarian assistance is adequately monitored and reaches those who need it most, the most vulnerable people of North Korea.

Mr. CHABOT. Thank you. Mr. Klingner, did you want to comment on that?

Mr. KLINGNER. Yes. H.R. 1771 certainly has an extensive list of actions that—I noticed a lot of overlap with my own recommendations.

I think, notably, on the human rights front, that is something that has lagged on the North Korean side, as we've seen legislation against Iranian human rights violations, Syrian. And I think just to go along sort of my theory of do unto North Korea as we have already done unto other violators of either human rights accords, or U.S. law, international law, U.N. resolutions.

So, I think—and a good starting point is look at the Commission of Inquiry's listing of the many North Korean Government entities or organizations that it condemns as being involved in these human rights violations. They should go on a U.S. sanctions list, not only the organizations themselves, but the individuals who head those organizations. I think that would be a very good starting point.

Mr. CHABOT. Thank you. This one is my last question. Ms. Jo, how do you assess the impact of foreign radio broadcasts from the U.S. and South Korea into North Korea? I think the administration favors increasing them and there's some question as to how effective they've been. How effective do you think they have been? Is there any way to make radio broadcasts into North Korea more effective? Did you ever hear anything like that? How old were you when you left, when you got out of North Korea?

Ms. JO. The last time was 16, 16-years-old.

Mr. CHABOT. Okay. Did you ever hear any radio broadcast coming in from outside of North Korea that said anything that would let you know what's really happening out there in the rest of the world? Did that ever happen?

Ms. JO. When I get international news or information is in China, yes.

Mr. CHABOT. From China. You didn't get anything from the U.S. or from South Korea that you're aware of then, I guess?

Ms. JO. Before we come to the United States.

Mr. CHABOT. Yes.

Ms. JO. We only watched the news about America. That's the only information we got from Chinese TV.

Mr. CHABOT. And that was from Chinese TV channels? Okay.

Ms. JO. Yes.

Mr. CHABOT. Okay, thank you. Okay. I'll turn the question over to you gentlemen then.

Mr. SCARLATOIU. Mr. Chairman, the company tasked to monitor broadcasting to North Korea, InterMedia, published a couple of years ago—back then, InterMedia was tasked to perform this mission, published an excellent report entitled, "A Quiet Opening." It conducted interviews with North Korean defectors, North Korean escapees. About one-third, 30 percent of them stated that they had listened to foreign broadcasting while in North Korea. Foreign broadcasting also includes broadcasting by stations based in South Korea.

For the past 10 years, we have seen a constant increase in the percentage of North Korean defectors who stated that they had listened to foreign broadcasting. Certainly, this does not necessarily mean that one-third of all people of North Korea listen to foreign broadcasting. These were those who were most likely to actively seek out information from the outside world, but North Korea is a country where radios have been sealed and basically set to one set government frequency. In the aftermath of the great famine of the 1990s, small informal markets have developed as a coping mechanism, not as the result of top down reform, and cheap radios have been available in these open markets, so more North Koreans have had access to radios, and to broadcasting stations based here in the United States, and also in South Korea.

Mr. CHABOT. Thank you. My time has actually expired. Mr. Klingner, did you want to add anything on the broadcasts into North Korea?

Mr. KLINGNER. Yes, if I could, sir. Information is one of the instruments of national power of the United States, along with diplomacy, military, economic, and other means. And getting information into North Korea I think is good. It's beneficial. It can have a corrosive effect on the regime. And we can do that through overt and covert means. Overt is through exchanges which are fine. We shouldn't oversell them as a substitute for conditional diplomatic engagement or more effective punitive measures.

We also should do it covertly. There's been a great deal of information that's gotten into North Korea through thumb drives, through pamphlets being transported by balloons, people bringing in DVDs and others. And that really shows the people of North Korea the reality of their own regime, as well as the reality of the outside world. So, I think we should do everything we can to encourage getting information in and out of North Korea through any means possible.

Mr. CHABOT. Thank you very much. As I said, my time is expired. We do have votes on the floor, but the gentleman from Virginia is recognized for up to 5 minutes.

Mr. CONNOLLY. I'll just ask one question as a follow-up if I may. Well, actually, two.

Mr. Klingner, with respect to the chairman's last question, you had been talking earlier about we ought to do unto North Korea what we've been willing to do to Iran. Do you think one of the reasons there's been some reluctance to do that is that one of the differences is Iran is sensitive to the impact of sanctions on its own population; whereas, North Korea seems to be utterly insensitive to the impact of sanctions or any other economic consequences, and is willing to have some percent of its own population starve to death, or suffer severe malnutrition rather than to bend the knee or relent. Is that—do you think that that may be one of the concerns the West has, that in inflicting punishment on a regime we're, in fact, directly inflicting punishment on innocent civilians?

Mr. KLINGNER. Actually, I think the reluctance to impose greater punitive measures on North Korea really is counterintuitive. As I said before, North Korea has withdrawn from the NPT. It's exploded nuclear devices. It says blatantly its nuclear program is for military purposes, and it also doesn't have a valuable commodity, oil, like Iran does. One would think there would be far greater sanctions on North Korea than Iran, but it's the opposite.

I think it's also useful to point out, though——

Mr. CONNOLLY. I guess what I'm getting at is why do you think that is so? And I'm offering you perhaps one theory for why it may be so, which in a strange way is a humanitarian reason.

Mr. KLINGNER. Right. But, actually, the targeted financial measures are not—would not impact the populace. They are not trade sanctions, they are not general sanctions. They are going after very specific financial links of the regime and other violators to the outside world. So, you know, I think the reluctance really is puzzling, not only to experts on North Korea, but particularly South Korean citizens who can't understand why the U.S. and the international community has been more reluctant to impose these things on North Korea. So, you know, it's targeted financial measures that we want, not broad sanctions that would impact the populous.

Mr. CONNOLLY. Yes. Thank you very much.

Mr. Scarlatoiu.

Mr. SCARLATOIU. Scarlatoiu, yes, sir.

Mr. CONNOLLY. Can you just briefly bring us up to date on one of the more bizarre practices of the North, and that is this whole phenomenon of abductees? It sounds to the uninitiated almost like a science fiction UFO kind of thing, abductees but, in fact, it's real.

Mr. SCARLATOIU. Congressman Connolly, thank you for the question. Our organization, the Committee for Human Rights in North Korea produced the only extensive English language report on this topic published 3 years ago entitled, ''Taken.'' One hundred and eighty thousand citizens of South Korea and other countries, including Japan and others have been taken by the North Koreans beginning on the 25th of June, 1950 when the North Korean military attacked South Korea. The practice goes back to a decree by Kim Il-sung. They initially intended to bring over the best and the brightest from South Korea to set up a new society. Most of them ended up in political prison camps. Ethnic Koreans from Japan who decided to return to North Korea, or were pushed to return at the time were never allowed to leave. Their Japanese spouses were not allowed to leave. There have also been foreign nationals of countries, including even, for example, Romania, former Communist ally of North Korea, who were taken, who were abducted by North Korean agents. They were forced to teach foreign languages and cultures to North Korean intelligence operatives. Their identities were used in North Korea's covert operations. And as I'm sure you recall, Congressman Connolly, in 1987, two North Korean agents bombed Korean Air Flight 858, before the 1988 Seoul Olympics. The two North Korean agents who bombed the plane posed as Japanese nationals, one of them, a woman, survived, sentenced to death. She survived, her sentence was commuted, married her bodyguard, became a star in South Korea, and told the story of how some of the Japanese abductees had provided training while she was in spy school.

Mr. CONNOLLY. It's an unbelievable story, and it deserves much more attention. Thank you for doing the only English report on this terrible practice. And, again, thank you to all of the panel for being with us today. Thank you, Mr. Chairman.

Mr. CHABOT. Thank you very much. The gentleman's time has expired. I also want to reiterate what the gentleman just said. I think this has been an excellent panel. We especially thank you, Ms. Jo, for having gone through this personally, and the trauma that you've suffered during the course of your life. Thank you, gentlemen, for devoting your lives to a critically important issue here. We appreciate it very much.

Members will have 5 days to submit questions, or to revise and expand any of their remarks. If there's no further business to come before the committee, we're adjourned. Thank you very much.

[Whereupon, at 4:09 p.m., the subcommittee was adjourned.]

APPENDIX

MATERIAL SUBMITTED FOR THE RECORD

SUBCOMMITTEE HEARING NOTICE
COMMITTEE ON FOREIGN AFFAIRS
U.S. HOUSE OF REPRESENTATIVES
WASHINGTON, DC 20515-6128

Subcommittee on Asia and the Pacific
Steve Chabot (R-OH), Chairman

March 25, 2014

TO: MEMBERS OF THE COMMITTEE ON FOREIGN AFFAIRS

You are respectfully requested to attend an OPEN hearing of the Committee on Foreign Affairs, to be held by the Subcommittee on Asia and the Pacific in Room 2172 of the Rayburn House Office Building (and available live on the Committee website at www.foreignaffairs.house.gov):

DATE: Wednesday, March 26, 2014

TIME: 2:00 p.m.

SUBJECT: The Shocking Truth about North Korean Tyranny

WITNESSES: Ms. Grace Jo
                   Survivor of North Korean human rights abuses

                   Mr. Greg Scarlatoiu
                   Executive Director
                   Committee for Human Rights in North Korea

                   Mr. Bruce Klingner
                   Senior Research Fellow
                   Northeast Asia
                   The Heritage Foundation

By Direction of the Chairman

The Committee on Foreign Affairs seeks to make its facilities accessible to persons with disabilities. If you are in need of special accommodations, please call 202/225-5021 at least four business days in advance of the event, whenever practicable. Questions with regard to special accommodations in general (including availability of Committee materials in alternative formats and assistive listening devices) may be directed to the Committee.

COMMITTEE ON FOREIGN AFFAIRS

MINUTES OF SUBCOMMITTEE ON _____ *Asia & the Pacific* _____ HEARING

Day __*Wednesday*__ Date _____*3/26/2014*_____ Room_____*2172*_____

Starting Time ____*2:06 pm*____ Ending Time ____*4:09 pm*____

Recesses | *1* | (*2:10pm* to *2:50pm*) (____to ____) (____to ____) (____to ____) (____to ____) (____to ____)

Presiding Member(s)
Chairman Steve Chabot (R-OH)

Check all of the following that apply:

Open Session ☑
Executive (closed) Session ☐
Televised ☑

Electronically Recorded (taped) ☑
Stenographic Record ☑

TITLE OF HEARING:
The Shocking Truth About North Korean Tyranny

SUBCOMMITTEE MEMBERS PRESENT:

Rep. Ami Bera (D-CA), Rep. Brad Sherman (D-CA), Rep. Dana Rohrabacher (R-CA), Rep. Scott Perry (R-PA), Rep. Gerald Connolly (D-VA), Rep. George Holding (R-NC)

NON-SUBCOMMITTEE MEMBERS PRESENT: *(Mark with an * if they are not members of full committee.)*

Chairman Ed Royce (R-CA)

HEARING WITNESSES: Same as meeting notice attached? Yes ☑ No ☐
(If "no", please list below and include title, agency, department, or organization.)

STATEMENTS FOR THE RECORD: *(List any statements submitted for the record.)*

TIME SCHEDULED TO RECONVENE _____
or
TIME ADJOURNED ___*4:09 pm*___

Subcommittee Staff Director